AF522042

MACHINE & ASSEMBLY LANGUAGE PROGRAMMING

No. 1389
$15.95

MACHINE & ASSEMBLY LANGUAGE PROGRAMMING

BY DAVID C. ALEXANDER

FIRST EDITION

THIRD PRINTING

Printed in the United States of America

Library of Congress Cataloging in Publication Data

Alexander, David C.
Machine and assembly language programming.

Includes index.
1. Assembler language (Computer program language) I. Title.
QA76.73.A8A345 1982 001.64'24 82-5831
ISBN 0-8306-2389-2 AACR2
ISBN 0-8306-1389-7 (pbk.)

This book is dedicated to

My loving wife Andrea who, while in ill health, devoted the time and patience to help me write it

My children—Annalece, Mike, Michelle, Billy, and Frank—for their help and patience

Dave, Fran, Steve, Ray, Don, and Isla who read the book and gave their opinions and encouragement, around which this course was designed

The member of my family who gave a week of his time to correct my terrible punctuation and spelling (I hope I didn't add to it later) and wishes to remain unnamed

To all a big THANKS!

Contents

	Introduction	ix
1	Numbering Systems	1
2	Why Use Machine and Assembly Language?	11
3	Registers, Register Pairs, and Addresses	13
4	Assembly Format	17
5	Operational Codes	23
6	The 8-Bit Load Group	27
7	The 16-Bit Load Group	37
8	Push and Pop	43
9	Exchanges, Block Transfers, and Search Group	51
10	The 8-Bit Arithmetic Group	65
11	General-Purpose Arithmetic and CPU Control Groups	77
12	The 16-Bit Arithmetic Group	83

13	The Rotate and Shift Group	89
14	Bit Set, Reset, and Test Group	97
15	The Jump Group	103
16	Call and Return Group	111
17	Pseudo-Ops	115
18	Sample Programs	123
19	BASIC to Machine: The Shapes Program	163
	Appendix A Codes	173
	Appendix B JR Suffixes	175
	Appendix C Numeric List of Machine Codes	177
	Appendix D Alphabetic List of Machine Codes	183
	Appendix E Reserved Words	191
	Glossary	193
	Index	197

Introduction

This book was written by a programmer who tried to learn machine and assembly language the hard way: on his own, without any help.

Do not read ahead unless you want to become totally lost and confused. This is a step-by-step learning method and *must* be followed as such. All of the materials tie in together. If you don't understand a chapter, read it again until you do.

Assembly language and machine language are like any other language. Computer languages can be compared to spoken language. All spoken languages do only one thing. They pass a thought or information from one person to another, regardless of whether they are spoken in English, Spanish, German, Russian, French, or any other language. For example: *buenas dias, bonjour*, and *hello* all do the same thing. They all express a greeting even though they are spoken in three different languages.

Programming is programming, regardless what language you use. A program does one thing, it passes information from one place to another, regardless of whether it's in English, BASIC, FORTRAN, COBOL, PL/I, machine, or assembly language.

This book assumes that you have had no experience whatsoever in programming and teaches you assembly and machine language. If you've had previous experience in programming, this book should make assembly and machine language that much easier. Most TRS-80 users start out programming in BASIC. If you've already studied BASIC, you know how easy it is.

After mastering this book, I recommend you read *TRS-80 Assembly Language Programming* by William Barden, Jr., available from Radio Shack (Cat. no. 62-2006). It is an excellent book for advanced machine- and assembly-language programming.

Should you have questions relating to my book, you may write to me at the following address; Dave Alexander, 220 West Second Street, Erie, PA 16507. Please send a self-addressed, stamped envelope.

Chapter 1
Numbering Systems

There are three main types of numbering systems that are used by computer programmers. They are the decimal, binary, and hexadecimal systems. The *decimal system* is based on powers of ten, and it is the one you have used all your life: 0 1 2 3 . . . 9.

Binary simply means powers of two. This system has only two numbers in it, zero and one.

The computer uses the binary system, or a version of it, in its operations. The variation is that a particular point within the memory is either positive (one) or negative (zero); more simply, the tiny electronic switching devices are either turned on or turned off.

As an assembly-language programmer, you won't write programs in binary, but it will be important for you to know how the binary system works.

Let's look at a number in binary and convert it to a decimal number. Let's take the binary number 11001. No, this is not eleven thousand one. Before I tell you what it really is, let's examine the decimal system briefly.

DECIMAL SYSTEM

A simple chart for finding powers of ten is given in Table 1-1. Remember that any number to the 0 power is one.

Table 1-1. Powers of 10.

Number	Power	Value
10	0	1
10	1	10
10	2	100
10	3	1,000
10	4	10,000
10	5	100,000
10	6	1,000,000
10	7	10,000,000
10	8	100,000,000
10	9	1,000,000,000
10	10	10,000,000,000

First let's look at the decimal number 25. That is to say ten to the power of zero, or 1 multiplied by 5 equals 5, and ten to the first power, or 10 multiplied by 2 equals 20.

2 × 10 to the 1st power (column 2)= 2 × 10 = 20
5 × 10 to the 0 power (column 1) = 5 × 1 = 5

Add the two and you get 25 for an answer.

```
 20        (column 2)
 +5        (column 1)
------
 25
```

Let's look at this in a different type of diagram.

Digit No.	2	1	
Decimal No.	2	5	
Multiplied by	(10) 1	(10) 0	
Answers	20	5	= 25

BINARY SYSTEM

Let's get back to our decimal conversion of the binary number 11001. Table 1-2 will help you to convert binary to decimal.

First, count the number of digits in the binary number and subtract 1. This will give you the highest power to be used. There are 5 binary digits in the number 11001, and when you subtract 1 from 5, you get 4.

Second, look up 4 on the binary chart in Table 1-2 (in the power column), and write down the corresponding number in the answer column. That's right. It is 16.

Third, look up the next lower number on the chart, the 3, and write down the corresponding decimal number for it. When you do this, you find that the answer is 8.

Fourth, look up the next lowest number on the chart, and write it down. We find that it is 0.

Fifth, look up the next lowest number on the chart, and write it down. It, too, is 0.

Sixth, look up the next lowest number on the chart, and write it down. It is 1. (Any number to the 0 power is 1.)

Seventh, add the answers: (16+8+0+0+1+0)=25

Let's look at this again, step by step.

Step 1. binary 11001 5 digits – 1 = 4 (the highest binary power to be used)
Step 2. from Table 1-2, the 4th power decimal value is 16.
Step 3. from Table 1-2, the 3rd power decimal value is 8.
Step 4. from Table 1-2, the 2nd power decimal value is 0.
Step 5. from Table 1-2, the 1st power decimal value is 0.
Step 6. from Table 1-2, the power decimal value is 1.
Step 7. add decimal values (16+8+0+0+1)=25

Here's an example for converting from the decimal system to the binary.

Step 1. Find the largest decimal number on the chart that does not exceed your number.
Step 2. Divide your decimal number by this value. If the answer is not 1 then you have used the wrong number from the chart.

Binary Power	Decimal Answer
0	1
1	2
2	4
3	8
4	16
5	32
6	64
7	128
8	256
9	512
10	1024

Table 1-2. Binary to Decimal Conversion.

Step 3. Multiply and subtract.
Step 4. From chart next lowest decimal value (remember all powers must be used in order whether it will go into the number or not).
Step 5. Divide this value into the remainder that you had in step 3 and repeat steps 3 - 4 - 5 until you have used all of the powers.

Now test yourself by finding the binary value of decimal number 25. Refer to Table 1-3.

I'll bet that you were surprised how easy it really was. Before we go any further, let's try some sample problems.

Convert the binary numbers to decimal numbers.

Binary to Decimal Conversion Problems

Problem No.	Binary No.	Decimal No.
1	11101	__________
2	11000	__________
3	111011	__________
4	11111111	__________
5	00001111	__________

Check your answers with those given at the end of the chapter. If your answers agree with those given, then go on to the next exercise. If they don't, recheck your work, and find your errors. The answers given are correct. If on reworking you cannot obtain the answer given, then reread this chapter. *Do not go any further until you have mastered this operation!*

Problem No.	Decimal No.	Binary No.
6	256	__________
7	376	__________
8	1087	__________
9	50743	__________
10	15360	__________

Check your answers with those on the following page. If your answers agree with those given, then go on to the next exercise. If they don't, recheck your work, and find your errors. The answers given are correct. If on reworking you cannot obtain the answer given, then reread this chapter. Do not go any further until you have mastered this operation!

Table 1-3. Binary Division.

Step Number	Decimal Value	Decimal Number	Binary Number	Math Operation
2	16	25 16 ----	1	Divide 25 by 16 Subtract
3	8	9 8 ----	1	Divide 9 by 8 Subtract
4	4	1 0 ----	0	Can't divide 1 by 4 Subtract
5	2	1 0 ----	0	Can't divide 1 by 2 Subtract
6	1	1 1 ---- 0	1	Divide 1 by 1 Subtract

7 Read the binary values down the binary = number column: 11001

HEXADECIMAL SYSTEM

Before you go on to hexadecimals, you may want to reread the binary section. If the binary system is clear to you, then you are ready for the hexadecimal numbering system, or hex as we will call it from now on.

This is the most important part of this book so far. This is because in machine and assembly language you will use hex constantly. Be sure you know this.

Hexadecimal or *hex* means base 16. The system numbers from 0 to 15, and never goes higher. That sounds too easy you say? What's the catch? Okay, you're right. There is a catch.

In hex, you can only have one-digit numbers so you can only use numbers from 0 to 9.

"So how do we get to 15," you ask. Well you begin using the alphabet after number 9. Let's see how hex compares to decimal.

Decimal:	0	1	2	3	4	5	6	7	8	9	10	11	12	13	14	15
Hex:	0	1	2	3	4	5	6	7	8	9	A	B	C	D	E	F

Table 1-4 will aid you in converting decimal to hex.

Now let's work a couple of problems with hex numbers. First let's change a decimal number to a hex number. Let's use the number 12,345 and convert it to hex. Look at Table 1-4 for hex to decimal numbers. Notice that there are four columns numbered left to right 4 to 1. Each column has two

Table 1-4. Decimal to Hexadecimal Conversion.

Column 4		3		2		1	
Hex	Dec	Hex	Dec	Hex	Dec	Hex	Dec
0	0	0	0	0	0	0	0
1	4,096	1	256	1	16	1	1
2	8,192	2	512	2	32	2	2
3	12,288	3	768	3	48	3	3
4	16,384	4	1,024	4	64	4	4
5	20,480	5	1,280	5	80	5	5
6	24,576	6	1,536	6	96	6	6
7	28,672	7	1,792	7	112	7	7
8	32,768	8	2,048	8	128	8	8
9	36,864	9	2,304	9	144	9	9
A	40,960	A	2,560	A	160	A	10
B	45,056	B	2,816	B	176	B	11
C	49,152	C	3,072	C	192	C	12
D	53,248	D	3,328	D	208	D	13
E	57,344	E	3,584	E	224	E	14
F	61,440	F	3,840	F	240	F	15

more columns inside it. These are called Hex and Dec. The decimal numbers are in the right of each column, and the hex numbers are in the left of each column.

To convert the number 12,345, or any decimal number, to hex follow these simple steps.

1. Look in column 4 and find the number that comes closest to 12,345, but does not exceed it. Then write down the hex number next to it. Subtract the decimal number from 12,345. In doing this we find that the decimal number in column 4 is 12,288. Write down the hex number (3) beside it. Now subtract: 12,345 – 12,288 = 57.

2. Next look in column 3 for the number 57. The smallest number in column 3 that we can subtract from 57, is 0. So we write down the hex number 0 and subtract: 57 – 0 = 57. Our hex number now reads 30.

3. Go to column 2 and find the number that is the closest to 57, but not larger than 57. There it is, 48. The hex number is 3. We write down the 3 making our hex number 303. Now subtract: 57 – 48 = 9.

4. The last step is simple. Look up the 9 in the decimal side of column 1. The hex number for 9 is 9, so we write this down, and our hex number now reads 3039.

But wait a minute. This is a hex number and since it doesn't have any letters in it, it looks like a decimal number. We have to label the number so as not to confuse it with decimal numbers. To do this, simply add the letter H. The H stands for hex, and since the largest hex digit is F, we can't mistake it for a digit. Our number now reads 3039H.

Now let's convert from hex to decimal. Let's use the number 3C0FH.

To change 3C0FH to decimal we find the 3 in column 4. We then write down the decimal number for the 3 in column 4 (12,288). Next we go to column 3 and find the C and write down the decimal for the C in column 3. We do the same thing for the last two digits so that our list of numbers reads: 12,288 3,072 0 & 15. Now add these numbers. 12,288 + 3,072 + 0 + 15 = 15,375. 3C0FH = 15,375. That's all there is to it.

Try a few of your own. You should look at the hex and decimal number arrangements, and compare them to the arrangements for binary. You should readily see how the hex numbers ascend in powers of 16. If you don't get the correct answers, reread the section on hex numbers and conversions.

Hex to Decimal Conversion Problems

Problem No.	Hex. No.	Decimal No.
1	3C00H	________
2	7FFFH	________
3	01C9H	________
4	0F0H	________
5	0FH	________

Problem No.	Decimal No.	Hex No.
6	32767	________
7	16360	________
8	0	________
9	10000	________
10	20480	________

Check your answers against those given at the end of the chapter.

QUIZ

1. Tell what type of numbering system the following represent.

   A. 110001001 ______________
   B. 3000H ______________
   C. 3000 ______________

2. Binary means base ______________
3. Hex means base ______________
4. Decimal means base ______________
5. Convert the following numbers to the two remaining systems.

	Decimal	Hex	Binary
A.	121	______	______
B.	______	39H	______
C.	______	______	10110
D.	1000	______	______
E.	______	FFH	______

Answers are given at the end of the chapter.

ANSWERS
Binary to Decimal Conversions

Problem No.	Answer	Procedure
1	29	11101 5 digits start at 4th power (16) 16+8+4+2+1 = 31
2	24	11000 5 digits start at 4th power (16) 16+8 0+0+0 = 24
3	59	111011 6 digits start at 5th power (32) 32+16+8+0+2+1 = 59
4	255	11111111 8 digits start at 7th power (128) 128+64+32+16+8+4+2+1 = 255
5	15	00001111 ** trick ** 4 actual digits. The leading zeros are not counted therefore there are only 4 digits so start at 3rd power (8) 8+4+2+1 = 15
6		100000000
7		101111000
8		10000111111
9		1100011000110111
10		11110000000000

Hex to Decimal Conversions

Problem No.	Answer	
1	15360	
2	32767	
3	457	
4	240	(Leading zeros are not counted and there should have been four digits so you had to add a leading zero)

5	15	
6	7FFFH	
7	3FE8H	
8	0000H	OR 00H
9	2710H	
10	5000H	

ANSWERS

Question No.	Answer	
1A.	Binary	
1B.	Hex	
1C.	Decimal	
2.	2	
3.	16	
4.	10	
5A.	79H	1111001
5B.	57	111011
5C.	22	16H
5D.	3E8H	1111101000
5E.	255	11111111

Chapter 2

Why Use Machine and Assembly Languages?

You may be wondering if it's really worth all the bother to learn to use machine and assembly language. Let me tell you a few things that you will find out about these languages as you go along.

Machine language addresses the CPU (central processing unit) directly. BASIC does not. Therefore it takes about 350 times longer to execute a program or a command in BASIC than it does in machine language. A good example of this is the one-second delay loop that you may have used in BASIC: FOR X = 1 TO 500 : NEXT. The same loop in machine language would not last one second. In machine language, the computer can count from 1 to 84,000 in one second. Now I know that 84,000/500 = 168, but there is time spent in overhead operations also. There are more instruction lines needed in machine and assembly language than in BASIC but less time is spent on overhead work and less memory required to write the program.

The main difference between BASIC and machine language is that a program written in BASIC must first be converted, one instruction at a time, by the computer into machine language so that the computer can understand it. In machine language, we are addressing the computer directly in its own language so no conversion is necessary.

Another feature of machine language makes sure that the program cannot be listed directly from the keyboard unless you have a program such as T-BUG, or Editor/Assembler. This offers greater security in business and confidential files. Listings can also be totally locked out by special program instructions that prevent loading of a program to list the instructions. This can make illegal copying of the program very difficult.

Along with these features is the convenience of locating subroutines, or subprograms in various areas of the main program, then going to these routines and back numerous times. You may have seen this done in BASIC to attempt to make alterations of the program more difficult. This works even better in machine language. As you will see later, or may have already, machine and assembly language programs are hard to follow unless you really understand the language. For this reason, you gain a security advantage over someone that doesn't really know the language.

In the next chapter we will begin to study programming commands and instructions. If at any time something is not clear to you reread it until you understand it.

Chapter 3
Registers, Register Pairs, and Addresses

In machine language we will be moving pieces of information around from one location to another. This process directly addresses the computer, which is about 300 times faster than BASIC.

Now let's stop here for a moment and go to the TRS-80 post office.

REGISTERS

When we walk in, we see a wall with many boxes on it. Let's call these boxes *registers.* Now, of course, there are many other TRS-80 post offices. You have one and so do I. You are in your post office, so that is your address or location. I am in mine, so that is my address or location. Also on the wall, in your post office, there is a big slot for mail. Let's call this a register. You have a letter, or some information, that you want to send to me, so you put it in the slot and the postman (the CPU) delivers it from your location to my location and puts it in my register.

We have just described the action that goes on inside the computer.

ADDRESSES

Let's explain *addresses.* These are memory locations in the computer. If you have a 16K machine, there are 32,767 memory locations in it. These are numbered from 000H to 7FFFH. Some of these locations are used by the computer for ROM (read-only memory) routines and housekeeping and must not be disturbed. These locations are from 0000H to 42E9H. Check the memory map in your owner's manual for these locations. It would also be a good idea to make a copy of the memory map and hang it near your terminal. You will refer to it constantly.

REGISTER TYPES

So much for that. Now the registers. There are eight registers. They are A, B, C, D, E, F, H, and L. These registers also have *primed* counterparts. These are A′, B′, C′, D′, E′, F′, H′, and L′. We will discuss these later. The important thing, at this point, is to know that they exist. There are also two other registers, X and Y, that we won't bother with now. These also have primed counterparts X′ and Y′.

Any single register can contain a value of up to 255 or FFH. To use a value larger than 255, you must pair two registers together to form a *register pair.* Registers may be paired in the following way: AF, BC, DE, and HL. These register pairs may also store values less than 255. The maximum value that can be stored in a register pair is 65,535 or FFFFH.

In addition to the four register pairs there are two *special register pairs*, IX and IY. There is also one more register pair called the sp register pair or *stack pointer.* It points to the top of the stack or the next address where information can be stored. We'll discuss the stack pointer later.

QUIZ

1. ____________ are memory locations in the computer.
2. The addresses from 0000h to 42E9H are referred to as ____________.
3. Name the eight registers.
4. Name the two special registers.
5. What are the primed registers?
6. List the register pairs.
7. List the special register pairs.
8. What is the largest value that can be stored in a register?
9. What is the largest value that can be stored in a register pair?
10. What is the SP register pair?

ANSWERS

1. addresses
2. ROM
3. A, B, C, D, E, F, H, L
4. X, Y
5. A′, B′, C′, D′, E′, F′, H′, L′
6. AF, BC, DE, HL
7. IX, IY
8. 255 (FFH)
9. 65535 (FFFFH)
10. stack pointer

Chapter 4
Assembly Format

Since we are just starting, it's best to see what we are doing, so we will use the Editor/Assembler to write our programs.

The Editor/Assembler is a program that allows us to write assembly-language programs, and then convert them to machine language. When we begin there will be five columns that we will be interested in. These are listed below.

Column 1	2	3	4	5
Line Number	**Label**	**Op-Code**	**Operand(s)**	**Comment**

After we assemble the program, there will be two more columns to the left of the first five. The resulting listing will look like this.

Col. 1	2	3	4	5	6	7
Memory Loc.	**Machine Code**	**Line No.**	**Label**	**Op-Code**	**Operand**	**Comment**

The difference between assembly language and machine language is simple. In assembly language we type in the instructions. The computer then takes these instructions and organizes them into machine code. If you are familiar with some of the larger computers, you know that they have a component called a *compiler*. The compilers translate a program into machine language all at once. Interpreters (commonly used for BASIC) translate the program into machine language one line at a time. Compilers are generally much faster. The Editor/Assembler works much like a compiler, however the compiler is in the assembler program only and is not part of the program that you write.

In machine language you will not type in the instructions in regular lines as you do in assembly language. Instead you insert the machine code (0s and 1s) in the memory locations that you want. You could spend a lot of time looking up the machine codes for a program. For this reason, until you get really good at it, we will use assembly language.

While you are learning assembly and machine language, I suggest you look at the machine codes in the seventh column of the assembled version of your programs. This will help you learn some of the codes, and aid you in learning how to write machine language programs.

If you have a T-BUG program and don't have an Editor/Assembler, I advise you to get one. This will help you when you try to write programs, as the machine codes are listed in a more easily readable form in the back of the Editor/Assembler manual.

Now, let's examine the columns that we just looked at. The first of the seven columns is labeled Memory Location. This tells us where the instruction is stored (its address). This number is always given in hex.

The next column is the Machine Code. This is the translated code that tells the computer what to do. For example: CDC901. We will find out what this instruction means later, but for now that's what a machine code instruction looks like.

The third column is the Line Number. Just as in BASIC, each line must have a number. Line numbers are useful in finding areas in the program after you have written a section. If you use certain line numbers for certain functions, when you need to add to the program, or find the area quickly, you can list the line numbers for that area. A good habit to get into is to allocate line number areas for certain functions. Then write down a key to the line numbers for reference. For example:

100-200 PRINT MENU
200-300 SEARCH FOR REQUESTED FUNCTION

The fourth column is the Label column. This column defines a function, or an area of the program that the program uses. *Labels must begin with a letter* and may be a combination of alphanumerics (letters and numbers) of up to 6 characters. A label must not contain the $ symbol, and ADD SUBINC EQU and DEC. These labels may be found in the Editor/ Assembler manual, or in the appendix in this book.

The fifth column is the Op-Code column. Op-Code is short for operation code. Its purpose is to tell the computer what kind of operation you want to perform.

There are various op-codes. Among them are LOAD, ADD, SUBTRACT, INCREMENT, DECREMENT, EXCHANGE, CALL, and JUMP. We will discuss these at length later. For now, don't worry about the commands. They are mentioned here only to give you an idea of what op-codes are.

There is also another type of op-code. It is called the Pseudo-Op. Pseudo-ops are special instructions that tell the computer to do special things. We will get into pseudo-ops later. For now you should know that there are nine pseudo-ops: ORG, EQU, DEFL, END, DEFB N, DEFB S, DEFW, DEFS, and DEFM.

The sixth column is the Operand column. The Operand is the register, register pair, or memory location that the operation is being performed on. For example, if I tell you to add, that's an op-code. You still don't know what to add to what. But if I tell you to add the contents of the "A" register to the contents of the "HL" register pair, then you know what to do. Here A and HL are the operands.

The seventh column is the Comment column. The comment tells us what we wanted the instruction to do. All entries to this column must be preceded by a *semicolon*. The semicolon separates the comment from the operand(s) and tells the computer to ignore the text of the comment.

You ask "Why do we need it?" Let me tell you a true story about what happened to me.

I had been working on a program to do some inventory control routines. After an hour of putting in the comment lines, I got tired of typing these useless lines, so I quit using them. Three hours later, at line 4,000, counting by tens, I needed to find a subroutine that I had used in a previous line. Since I had no comment lines to guide me, it took me two hours to find what I wanted. Since then I used them religiously. You can always take them out when you are done, but having them can save a lot of time and trouble.

QUIZ

1. ________ are a group of letters and numbers that may be used as a label.
2. The memory location is always given in ________.
3. The ________ tells the computer what to do.
4. ________ are used in all lines and can be used to divide the program into sections.
5. ________ are used to mark a subroutine.
6. The ________ tells the computer what kind of function to perform.
7. The ________ is a special op-code.
8. The ________ tells what the op code is being performed on.
9. ________ should be used in each line to tell you what you are doing in that line.

ANSWERS

1. alphanumerics
2. hex
3. machine code
4. line numbers
5. labels
6. op-code
7. pseudo-op
8. operand
9. comments

Chapter 5
Operational Codes

The last chapter briefly discussed what op-codes do, and what they are. Now we will get down to what the various op-codes are, and what they do. Remember, this is a book for beginners, so I will not go into things in detail. I will give you a fundamental understanding of what is what. You can further your education through books that are already on the market.

It might be advisable to learn a little about the computer's memory. If you will picture a stack of boxes in your mind, it will be easier. The boxes represent memory locations. There will be one box for each location. The stack of boxes represent the ***memory stack***, or ***stack***, as we call it. A stack is nothing more than a group of memory cells piled one on top of the other.

The computer stack is a LIFO (last in first out) operation. Picture a man climbing up a stack of boxes. As he goes up, he puts a paper in each one of the boxes. However, to get down on the floor again, he must climb down. As he climbs down, he must take the paper from each of the boxes on his way. Therefore, the last paper he put in the boxes will be the first one that he takes out. The first one that he put in will be the last one that he takes out.

The stack is usually defined as the available memory above the last program instruction. There are two exceptions, however.

The first exception is that a program can contain what is called an *internal stack.* This is an area inside the program that is used to store information temporarily. The second exception is that if a program is located in the middle of the memory, you can use the available space below the program for a stack. This area is called a *buffer.* A buffer is a temporary storage area.

From this point on you will begin to learn about the different op-codes, and a little about how they are used.

From now on, you must recognize and know the following abbreviations.

N	Number. Any hex or decimal from 0 to 32767
R	Any single register
R′	Any single primed register
RR	Any register pair
RR′	Any primed register pair

The first op-code, load, is covered in the next two chapters. Then we'll move onto the op-codes *push* and *pop.* These are used to save and retrieve information.

Other op-codes include *exchanges, block transfers, searches, loads with decrements and increments, adds, subtracts, logical ands, and ors, decrements, increments, rotates, shifts, bit sets, and resets, jumps, calls, and returns.* These are covered in later chapters.

QUIZ

1. What does LIFO mean?
2. The ________ is the available memory above the last program instruction.
3. A __________ is sometimes called an internal stack.
4. If the top of the stack is 7000H, and the bottom of the same stack is 6000H, what will the address for the next available stack location be?

ANSWERS

1. last in first out
2. stack
3. buffer
4. 7001H

Chapter 6
The 8-Bit Load Group

Now let's look at the first op-code, *LD*. LD stands for Load. This command tells the computer to load a register, register pair, or a memory location with a value. This value can be supplied by you from the keyboard, inside the program, from another register, or a memory location. As a general definition, load means to *store* information.

There are two types of loads. An 8-bit load and a 16-bit load; which is covered in the next chapter.

8-BIT LOADS

A *bit* is the smallest unit in a memory location. There are 8 bits to a byte. A *byte* is one letter, number, space or item of punctuation. A byte can be thought of as a memory location.

To study the various op-codes, we will include the operands, to give you an idea of the various types of functions that can be carried out by the op-codes.

A good rule of thumb to use when determining what type of load you're dealing with, is that 8-bit loads use single registers. We will format the op-codes in the following manner.

op-code   operand

Now for the 8-bit loads. The first 8-bit load will tell us to load R,R′.

LD R,R′

In this instruction the register (R) is loaded with the contents of its primed counterpart, (R′). For example, if the H register contains 05H, and the H′ register contains 10H, after LD H,H′ is executed, both registers will contain 10H.

Before LD R,R′

Register	Contents	Register	Contents
H	05H	H′	10H

After LD R,R′

Register	Contents	Register	Contents
H	10H	H′	10H

Now suppose that we want to load one register with the value of another register.

LD R,R

Say that the A register contains 0FH, and the H register contains 2FH. After executing LD AH, the A register and the H register will both contain 2FH. This can also be done using primed registers. Following is an example of two ways to do this.

```
LD    A,H
LD    A′,H′
```

Before LD R,R

Register	Contents	Register	Contents
A	05H	H	10H
A′	15H	H′	25H

After LD R,R

Register	Contents	Register	Contents
A	10H	H	10H
A′	25H	H′	25H

The next command will tell us to load a given register with a number value. Number values for single registers may not exceed 255 or FFH. However you may load in either decimal or hex numbers. If the H is not put in the number, the computer will treat the number as decimal. Great care should be exercised when doing this as there is a lot of difference between 10 decimal and 10H. Also, if you attempt to load the number 8A, and forget the H, the computer will print an error message. This load command looks like this;

LD R,N

In this case, if the A register contains 04H, and you want it to contain 0FH, you would execute this command; LD A,0FH. After this is executed, the contents of the A register will be 0FH.

Before LD R,N

Register	Contents
A	04H

After LD R,N

Register	Contents
A	0FH

Now, suppose you want to load a register with the contents of a memory location. This can get a little difficult, so pay close attention. You remember that a register can contain numbers up to 255, and that for numbers greater than 255, you have to use register pairs.

Let's say that the HL register pair contains the number 3C00H. 3C00H is actually a memory location and is larger than 255, or FFH, therefore it would appear that you cannot load it into a single register.

However, you want the contents of HL loaded into the A register. You can do this by enclosing the HL in parentheses like this (HL). This tells the computer to load the contents of the register pair, not the value stored in the register pair. 3C00H is the starting address for the video memory. Let's say that the first character displayed on the screen is the letter E. The ASCII code for E is 45H. (We'll discuss ASCII codes later, but for now all we need to know is that memory location 3C00H contains the value 45H.)

Location	Contents	Register Pair	Contents
3C00H	45H	HL	3C00H

Here's the tricky part. The HL register pair contains 3C00H, and location 3C00H contains 45H. Therefore the value transferred by loading the A register with the contents of the HL register pair, (HL), is 45H, not 3C00H. The command is like this:

LD A, (HL)

Before LD A,(HL)

HL	Location 3C00H	A Register
3C00H	45H	10H

After LD A, (HL)

HL	Location 3C00H	A Register
3C00H	45H	45H

Let's say that the A register contains the value 10H. After we execute the instruction LD A,(HL) the A register will contain 45H, and HL will still contain 3C00H, while the contents of 3C00H will still be 45H.

The previous command can be used for any of the registers. In the case above we would not use the H or L registers, as this would change the value of the register pair.

Now for the special registers, IX and IY. The same rule applies to these registers as it did in the previous example. There is one difference. These registers can show a displacement value with the command. Now let's say that the IX register pair contains 3C00H and the contents of 3CFFH is 20 (the ASCII code for a space).

The command for the IX and IY registers looks like this.

```
LD  R, (IX+D)
LD  R, (IY+D)
```

The D in the example denotes the displacement. The displacement is the number of bytes beyond the address pointed to by the IX or IY register pair. However, if there is no displacement, the displacement symbol may be omitted. Therefore after you execute the command LD A,(IX+FFH) the contents of the A register will be 20H, the IX register will contain 3C00H, and 3CFFH will still contain 20H. You can express the displacement in decimal form too.

Next let's load a value into a memory location. This could be in the stack, in a buffer, or on the screen. Let's load an E into the first position on the screen, 3C00H. Right now let's say that 3C00H contains 20H, a space. Let's say that the A register (the *accumulator*) now has the value 45H, the D, and that the DE register pair contains 3C00H. The command looks like this:

LD (RR),R

Before LD (RR),R:

Register Pair	Contents	Location	Contents	A Register Contents
DE	3C00H	3C00H	20H	45H

After LD (RR),R

Register Pair	Contents	Location	Contents	A Register Contents
DE	3C00H	3C00H	45H	45H

Exchanging the R's for the registers, we have LD (DE),A. Upon executing this command, the A register will still contain 45H. The DE register pair will still contain 3C00H, but location 3C00H will now contain 45H. The result will be that the letter E will be displayed at the start of the screen. Later on we will play with this, and use it to display various things on the screen.

The next thing we will do is to load the contents of the two special register pairs, IX and IY, with the contents of another register. We will do this in the same way that we did in the last example, and the commands will look like this:

```
LD      (IX+D),R
LD      (IY+D),R
```

The results are the same as the LD (DE),A command and the (IX+D) is treated the same as in the LD R,(IX+D) command that we already discussed. An example follows:

Before LD (IX+D),R
LD (IY+D),R:

Register Pair	Contents	Location	Contents
IX	3C00H	3C00H	20H
IY	3C50H	3C50H	41H

A Register Contents	Displacement
45H	10H

Location	Contents	Location	Contents
3C10H	50H	3C60H	49H

After LD (IX+D),R
LD (IY+D),R

Register Pair	Contents	Location	Contents
IX	3C00H	3C00H	20H
IY	3C50H	3C50H	41H

A Register Contents	Displacement
45H	10H

Location	Contents	Location	Contents
3C10H	45H	3D60H	45H

There are two other possible ways to load the accumulator (A) register with the contents of a memory location. We know that we can load A with the contents of the HL register pair, LD A,(HL). Now let's look at the other two ways.

```
LD      A,(DE)
LD      A,(BC)
```

Note that these are the same as the LD R,(RR) command.

Now let's see how we can load a value directly from a memory location into the accumulator. This is done by using the following command:

```
LD      A,(NN)
```

In the following example let's say that the A register contains 50H, location 3C00H contains 45H, and we want to load the accumulator with the value stored in 3C00H. The proper command is:

```
LD      A,(3C00H)
```

Location	Contents	Register	Contents
3C00H	45H	A	50H

After we execute this command, the contents of 3C00H will still be 45H, and the contents of the accumulator will be 45H.

Location	Contents	Register	Contents
3C00H	45H	A	45H

This step would be useful, for example, to take the information on the screen and send it to the printer.

Just about anything can be loaded into the accumulator. You should remember that earlier we loaded the A register with the contents of the DE register pair. We can also load the contents of the HL register pair, and the contents of the BC register pair with the contents of the A register. These commands do that.

```
LD      (HL),A
LD      (BC),A
```

We can also load a memory location with the contents of the A register. Here's how that looks:

```
LD      (NN),A
```

OR:

```
LD      (42EAH),A
```

Here are examples of these commands, given the fact that the A register contains 52H. The following examples will be in the same order that we have already discussed them.

Before

Register	Contents	Location	Contents
HL	5000H	5000H	FFH
BC	5A00H	5A00H	23H

After

Register	Contents	Location	Contents
HL	5000H	5000H	52H
BC	5A00H	5A00H	52H

You can see that in the 8-bit load group the contents of the register, register pair, memory location, or *the number to the right of the comma* are loaded into the location, register, or register pair *on the left of the comma*.

There are four more loads in the 8-bit load group. We won't explain them in this book, but we will show them to you. I consider these four to be beyond the beginner stage, and you won't be using them for a while anyway. The four loads:

LD	A,I	Load the accumulator with the contents of the interrupt vector.
LD	A,R	Where R= the contents of the memory refresh.
LD	I,A	Load the interrupt control vector with the contents of the accumulator.
LD	R,A	Where R=the memory refresh register, and the contents of the accumulator are loaded into it.

Don't worry about interrupts and refresh in this book, but do note that the accumulator is the A register.

QUIZ

1. What does LD mean?
2. ____________ means to store information.
3. A ____________ is smallest unit in a memory location.
4. There are 8 ____________ in a ____________.
5. Show how to load the A register with the contents of the A′ register.
6. Show how to load the A register with FFH.
7. Show how to load the A register with the contents of the HL register pair.
8. Give the contents of the HL register pair, the contents of the location pointed to by the HL register pair, and the contents of the A register after the instruction LD A,(HL) given these conditions:
   - A. The HL register pair contains 3C00H
   - B. The contents of 3C00H is 41H
   - C. The A register

ANSWERS

1. load
2. load
3. bit
4. bits byte
5. LD A,A′
6. LD A,FFH
7. LD A,(HL)
8. HL will contain 3C00H
   3C00H will contain 41H
   The A register will contain 41H

Chapter 7
The 16-Bit Load Group

Having mastered the 8-bit load group, you are now ready to tackle the 16-bit load group. Don't think that it is more difficult than the 8-bit load group. It isn't.

The 16-bit load group deals with register pairs instead of single registers, and in this group we will deal with a new register pair, the *SP register pair*. It is the register pair that continually points to the top of the stack. For this reason we call it the SP or *stack pointer* register pair.

In this chapter you will notice the absence of the AF register pair in the load commands. This is because the A register will be used to accumulate and transfer information to the other register pairs, and the F register is used as a flag to show various conditions. We'll study the flag conditions later. By the way, there is another little convenience, the F register carries the FLAG condition. Remember F for FLAG.

The first load is the one that loads a 2-byte integer into a register pair. This integer, or number, can be as little as 0, or as great as 65535 (FFFFH).

The code for this load is:

```
LD      RR,NN
```

Where RR is any one of the BC, DE, HL, or SP register pairs, and NN is the integer.

Let's see what happens in this instruction if NN = 3C00H and RR = the DE register pair.

LD DE,3C00H

After this instruction is executed, the contents of the DE register pair will be 3C00H, and the contents of location 3C00H will be unchanged. An example follows.

Before

Reg. Pair	Contents	Location	Contents
DE	4000H	3C00H	45H

After

Reg. Pair	Contents	Location	Contents
DE	3C00H	3C00H	45H

The next instruction is

LD IX,NN.

This instruction tells the computer to load the IX register pair with the integer NN. Also, the computer will load the first N into the *low order* of the BYTE. Therefore if NN = 7FFFH

LD IX,7FFFH,

will cause the IX register pair to contain 7FFFH. The same holds true for the IY register pair, and they both act the same as the previous command that we just discussed.

Now, let's suppose that we want to load the contents of a memory location into a register pair. We can do this by using any of the BC, DE, HL, or SP register pairs. Let's load the HL register pair with the contents of location 4000H. The command looks like this:

LD HL, (4000H)

or

LD RR, (NN)

Let's pause a moment and think about this. We know that there are 8 bits to a byte. We also know that one byte is one memory location, so there are 8 bits to a memory location. But we have just done a 16-bit load. That has to mean that we've loaded the contents of two locations into one register pair. Tell me what went where. (Hint: I used the HL register pair to make it easy to remember.)

As this was a 16-bit load, the contents were peeled off the stack last in first out. Therefore, the H register will contain the high order of the load, and the L register will contain the low order. Remember H for High, and L for Low.

Let's do this again, only let's look at the contents of the HL register pair after the command is executed. Say that location 4000H contains 20H, and location 4001H contains 45H. After we execute this command, the H register will contain the 45H that it got from location 4001H, and the L register will contain the 20H that it got from location 4000H. An example follows.

Before

Register	Contents	Location	Contents
H	30H	4000H	20H
L	41H	4001H	52H

After

Register	Contents	Location	Contents
H	52H	4000H	20H
L	20H	4001H	52H

Don't get the idea that the HL register pair stands for high/low, or that the HL register pair is the only register pair that can be used this way. I merely used the HL for this example hoping that you will remember the example in the future and use it as a key when you get stumped with other register pairs or similar situations. It is always a good idea to learn these little ways to remember these procedures. Quite often, when you are writing tough or long programs, you will become tired or confused by the laws of machine language. At these times, little aids will help you to keep a clear head.

Now that you know how to load the contents of a memory location into a register pair, how do you think you load the contents of a register pair into a memory location? Think about it for a minute.

```
LD      (NN),HL
```

Again, to make it simple, we'll use the HL register pair. The command LD will be first. Next, enclose the memory location in brackets, separate them by a comma, and enter the location.

The contents of the L register will be loaded into the memory location. Where will the contents of the H register go? Into the memory location + 1 or the next highest location, as follows.

Before LD (4000H),HL

Register	Contents	Location	Contents
H	30H	4000H	20H
L	41H	4001H	52H

After

Register	Contents	Location	Contents
H	30H	4000H	41H
L	41H	4001H	30H

Once again remember HL. The HL register pair is not the only register pair that can be used to transfer information to a memory location. We can also use the BC, DE, SP, IX, and IY register pairs in exactly the same way. We can also load register pairs directly from other register pairs.

This method is limited to three different register pairs that are able to load one register pair. The three register pairs are the HL, IX, and IY. These can be loaded directly into the SP register pair only.

```
LD    SP,HL
LD    SP,IX
LD    SP,IY
```

In these instructions, the SP register pair is loaded with the contents of the other register pair. Then the contents of both pairs will be the same.

QUIZ

1. Show how to load the HL register pair with the contents of the DE register pair.
2. Show how to load the HL register pair with 3C00H.
3. Show how to load the DE register pair with the contents of 3C00H.
4. Give the contents of the HL register pair, the contents of the location pointed to by the HL register pair, and the contents of the DE register pair after the instruction LD DE,(HL) given these conditions:
   A. The HL register pair contains 3C00H
   B. The contents of 3C00H is 41H
   C. The DE register contains FFH

ANSWERS

1. LD HL,(DE)
2. LD HL,3C00H
3. LD DE,(3C00H)
4. HL will contain 3C00H
   3C00H will contain 41H
   the DE register pair will contain 41H

Chapter 8
Push and Pop

In the last chapter we talked a little about the SP register pair and mentioned that it was the stack pointer. Let's look at one of the functions of the stack pointer.

STACK POINTER

Let's say that we have a value stored in the HL register pair, and that we want to save it and use the HL register pair again. We could store the value in the HL register pair in a memory location, or another register pair. However let's say that all of the other register pairs are needed, and there is no room in the internal buffer in our program. Also imagine that we have no external buffer set up; and that we don't know where the top of the stack is.

First, let's straighten the stack out in our minds. The top of the stack is the *first memory location available that is not used by the program.* This does not mean that if you have a 16K machine, and the last location used by the program is 5000H, that the top of the stack is at 5001H. In this case the top of the stack is at 7FFFH because the stack has not been used yet. Since it is a LIFO operation, it will build down, not up. The bottom of the stack will be 7FFFH, and the top of the usable stack would be 5001H when and if we loaded the entire stack.

However, if we move something to the top of the stack at this point, it would go into 7FFFH, then 7FFEH. The next location available would be 7FFDH, and the SP register pair would be pointing to 7FFEH. One other very important thing to learn at this point is that the SP always points to the last location used, and when it is called upon to perform a function, it is decremented (lowered by one, or has one subtracted from it).

PUSH

Now back to the first problem. Let's say that the HL register pair contains the value 1050H. The H register contains 50H and the L register holds 10H. We can save this value by using the PUSH command. It will look like this;

PUSH HL

Before this command is executed, let's say that the SP register pair is pointing to 700AH. After this command, location 7009H will contain 10H and location 7008H will contain 50H. The SP register pair will be pointing to 7008H. Study the following:

Before PUSH HL (if HL contains 1050)

Location	Contents	Location	Contents
7009H	00H	7008H	00H

After

Location	Contents	Location	Contents
7009H	50H	7008H	10H

Let's look at this again. When we started, the SP register pair was pointing to 700AH. The PUSH command decremented the SP so that it then pointed to 7009H. At that time, the contents of the L register were loaded into 7009H. The SP register pair was again decremented, and was then pointing to 7008H. At that time, the contents of the H register was loaded into 7008H. Remember, this was a LIFO operation. By the way, the BC, DE, HL, AF, IX, and IY register pairs can be pushed onto the stack.

POP

Now that we have the contents of the HL register stored in the stack, how do we get it back? We just POP it back.

POP HL

After we POP HL, the contents of HL will be 1050H. When we told the computer to POP HL, it moved the stack pointer to the first location that it had PUSHed information to, loaded the L register with the contents of that location, then decremented the SP, and loaded the H register with the contents of that location. Here's what happens:

Before POP HL (if HL contains 4000H)

Location	Contents	Location	Contents
7009H	50H	7008H	10H
Register	Contents	Register	Contents
H	40H	L	00H

The stack pointer contains 7008H

After

Location	Contents	Location	Contents
7009H	50H	7008H	10H
Register	Contents	Register	Contents
H	10H	L	50H

The stack pointer contains 700AH

Instant replay. The SP is pointing to 7008H. The instruction POP HL is encountered. The SP moved back to 7009H. The contents of 7009H were 50H. The 50H was then loaded into the L register. The SP was then moved to 7008H. The contents of 7008H was 10H. The H register was loaded with 10H. The contents of the HL register was then 1050H.

When the computer PUSHed the HL register pair, it *did not* make any notations as to what it PUSHed. That is, it didn't say, "This is the area that I PUSHed the HL into". This makes it necessary for you to keep track of the order you PUSH and POP information in the program. If you don't, you may find that you are not getting the information back where you want it.

For example, it is possible to PUSH more than one register pair without POPPING the others out of the stack. If you PUSH HL, then PUSH DE, and the SP register was pointing to 700AH before you PUSHED HL, this is what happens. The contents of the H register will be stored in 7009H, L will be in 7008H, D will be in 7007H, and E will be in 7006H. The SP will be pointing to 7006H. Now, when you POP any register, the SP will move to 7006H and load the contents of 7006H and 7007H into that register pair.

This could present problems. For example:

```
PUSH    HL
PUSH    DE
```

Register	Contents	Location	Contents
H	C9H	7009H	C9H
L	01H	7008H	01H
D	3CH	7007H	3CH
E	00H	7006H	00H

Then if you;

```
POP    HL
POP    DE
```

Register	Contents	Location	Contents
E	C9H	7006H	C9H
D	01H	7007H	01H
L	3CH	7008H	3CH
H	00H	7009H	00H

The contents of the DE register pair will be what was originally stored in the HL register pair, and the contents of the HL register pair will be what was originally in the DE register pair. If you want to reverse the contents of the register pairs, however, the proper way is

```
PUSH    HL
PUSH    DE
```

Then

```
POP    DE
POP    HL
```

This is the way that you must do it to retrieve the data in the correct order. It is not necessary to POP the register pairs at the same time. However, you can POP one pair, then perform a few functions, then POP the next one.

QUIZ

1. __________ means to save the value in a register pair on the top of the stack.
2. __________ means to retrieve information from the top of the stack.
3. Give the correct order to retrieve the DE and HL register pairs after PUSH HL PUSH DE
4. Show how to put the value in the HL register pair in the DE register pair, and the value in the DE register pair in the HL register pair using PUSH and POP.

ANSWERS

1. PUSH
2. POP
3. POP DE POP HL
4. PUSH DE PUSH HL

   POP DE POP HL

Chapter 9
Exchanges, Block Transfers, and Search Group

In the last chapter we discussed how to use PUSH and POP to exchange the contents of one register pair with another. We could also have done this using various combinations of LOAD commands. Now we will learn the easy way to do it using the EXCHANGE command.

EXCHANGE

The EXCHANGE command we will be using is only valid in certain instances. Let's look at the first one.

```
EX          DE,HL
```

In this command, the contents of the HL register pairs, and the DE register pairs are EXCHANGED or swapped. Here's an example: If the HL register pair contains the number 1000H, and the DE register pair contains the number 5025H, after the command EX DE,HL the DE register pair will contain 1000H, and the HL register pair will contain 5025H. It's important to note that the original contents of the H register was 10H, and the original contents of the L register was 00H. Also, the original contents of the D register was 50H and the E register was 25H.

Register	Contents	Register Pair	Contents
H	10H	HL	1000H
L	00H		
D	50H	DE	5025H
E	25H		

After the EXCHANGE command, the contents of the H register are 50H, and the L register contains 25H. The D register now contains 10H, and the E register contains 00H.

Register	Contents	Register Pair	Contents
D	10H	DE	1000H
E	00H		
H	50H	HL	5025H
L	25H		

What I am trying to show is that the H and D registers are EXCHANGED and the L and E registers are exchanged.

The next EXCHANGE that we will look at is the EX AF,AF' command. In this command the contents of the AF register pair are EXCHANGED with it's primed counter part, AF'. The contents of the A register are EXCHANGED with the contents of the A' register, and the contents of the F register are EXCHANGED with the contents of the F' register. For example, if the contents of the AF register pair is 4350H, and the contents of the AF' register pair is 5025H, then after the command

```
EX          AF,AF'
```

the contents of the AF register will be 5025H, and the contents of the AF' register pair will be 4350H. These exchanges are easy, but you must remember two things about them. First, they can only be used between certain register pairs. These are listed in this chapter, and in the editor/assembler manual. Second, the EX command only affects the register pairs, not the contents of them. If the HL register pair contains 3C00H, and location 3C00H contains 20H, and the DE register pair contains 4000H, and location 4000H contains 2EH, then after the command

```
EX          DE,HL
```

the HL register pair will contain 4000H, and location 4000H will still contain 2EH. The DE register pair will now contain 3C00H, and location 3C00H will still contain 20H. Again, note that the EX command affects only the contents of the register pairs, and did not alter the contents of the locations stored in those register pairs.

The next EXCHANGE command is the EXX command. This one is generally used in only very special applications. The command looks like this:

EXX

Note that there is no operand following this command. This command tells the computer to EXCHANGE the contents of the BC register pair with it's primed counterpart, and at the same time to EXCHANGE the DE register pair with its primed counterpart, and also to EXCHANGE the HL register pair with its primed counterpart.

Let's diagram this with a chart. Let's say that the chart below contains the values of the BC, DE, HL, BC', DE', and HL' register pairs.

(BC)	(BC')	(DE)	(DE')	(HL)	(HL')
1000H	1010H	2000H	2020H	3000H	3030H

Now after the command, EXX

(BC)	(BC')	(DE)	(DE')	(HL)	(HL')
1010H	1000H	2020H	2000H	3030H	3000H

As you can see from the chart, the contents of the register pairs are EXCHANGED only with their primed counterparts. No EXCHANGE takes place between the HL, DE, and BC register pairs.

The next command also has limited and special usage. This command EXCHANGEs the contents of the Stack Pointer with the contents of the HL, IX, or IY register pairs.

```
EX      (SP),HL
EX      (SP),IX
EX      (SP),IY
```

Again we are performing a simple EXCHANGE, but with certain conditions. The contents of the L register are EXCHANGEd with the contents of the memory location specified by the SP (stack pointer) register pair, and the contents of the H register are EXCHANGEd with the next highest address above the stack pointer. Let's look at this EXCHANGE given the following information:

The contents of the HL register pair is 3C00H.
The SP register pair contains 7000H.
Location 7000H contains 67H.
Location 7001 contains 32H.

If this is true, then executing the instruction EX (SP),HL will result in the following:

The HL register pair will contain 3267H.
Memory location 7000H will contain 00H.
Memory location 7001H will contain 3CH.
The SP register pair will contain 7000H.

The same would be true if we had used the IX or IY register pairs instead of the HL register pair.

BLOCK TRANSFERS

Now let's look at a fast way to EXCHANGE and load the contents of register pairs. This is done by using BLOCK TRANSFERS. In a BLOCK TRANSFER, information is passed from one register pair to another. Then certain register pairs are incremented (advanced one memory location), and the contents of others are decremented (decreased by one).

The first one that we will look at is the LDI instruction. It will appear in a program in the following manner:

LDI

Note that no operand exists after the LDI op-code. This is true for all of the BLOCK TRANSFERS. The reason being that a BLOCK TRANSFER instruction automatically tells the computer what to do. It also means that you are limited to what can be transferred by using the TRANSFER instruction. In the case of the LDI instruction, a byte of data is transferred from the memory address pointed to by the HL register pair to the address pointed to by the DE register pair. Then the HL register pair and the DE register pair are advanced one memory location. At the same time, the contents of the BC (byte counter) register pair is decremented.

Let's replay the sequence.

Let's set up the following conditions. Say that the DE register pair contains 3C00H, the start of the video screen. Imagine there is nothing on the screen, or that it is filled with spaces. The code for a space is 20H.

So location 3C00H, 3C001H, 3C002H, and so on, all contain 20H. Now we want to print on the screen the contents of locations 5000H, 5001H, 5002H, which contain the codes of locations 5000H, 5001H, 5002H, which contains the codes for the first three letters of the alphabet, A, B, and C. The codes for these letters are 41H, 42H, and 43H. Therefore, 5000H contains 41H, 5001H contains 42H, and 5003H contains 43H. Now we want to print three letters. We do this by telling the BC (byte counter) register pair that we want the instruction repeated three times. Therefore, we will have already loaded the BC register pair with 03H.

Now we execute the LDI command. This causes the following things to happen:

The contents of 5000H (41H) are put into location 3C00H.
The DE register pair is moved up to 3C01H.
The HL register pair is moved up to 5001H.
The Byte Counter (BC) is decremented by one.

Now the contents of 3C00H is 41H, 3C01H is 20H, and 3C02H is 20H. The contents of location 5000H is 41H, 5001H is 42H, and 5002H is 43H. The byte counter (BC) register pair now has 02H in it.

After the entire instruction has been completed, we will have this:

The contents of the BC register pair will be 02H.
The contents of the HL register pair will be 5001H.
The contents of the DE register pair will be 3C01H.
The contents of the memory addresses will be as follows:

Location	Contents	Location	Contents
3C00H	41H	5000H	41H
3C01H	20H	5001H	42H
3C02H	20H	5002H	43H
3C03H	20H		

Note that the instruction was not repeated. The contents of the BC register pair is now 02H, and not 00H. The next instruction will repeat the command.

Let's look at the LDIR instruction. This instruction has no operand. The operand is understood to be the same as the LDI instruction with one major addition. It will be repeated until the contents of the BC register pair is zero. Using the information that we used for the LDI command, let's examine what happens with the LDIR command.

We already know that the process will be repeated three times since the contents of the byte counter was three.

Location	Contents	Location	Contents
3C00H	41H	5000H	41H
3C01H	42H	5001H	42H
3C02H	43H	5002H	43H
3C03H	20H		

The BC register pair contains 00H.
The DE register pair contains 3C03H.
The HL register pair contains 5003H.

As in the LDI command, the contents of the locations pointed to by the HL register pair are unaltered.

Let's look at the next instruction, LDD. This instruction is similar to the LDI instruction except that with LDD, the register pairs are all decremented. Using the same values for the contents of the memory locations, and the register pairs, let's see what the LDD command produces. After the first execution, we see:

Location	Contents	Location	Contents
3C00H	41H	5000H	41H
3C01H	20H	5001H	42H
3C02H	20H	5002H	43H

The contents of HL will be 4FFFH.
The contents of DE will be 3BFFH.
The contents of BC will be 02H.

Note that the contents of all the register pairs were decremented while the same results were produced. Let's do it again and change a few more things around.

First change the contents of DE from 3C00H to 3C02H. Next change the contents of HL from 5000H to 5002H. We'll leave the contents of BC at 03H, and the contents of the locations 3C00H to 3C03H, and 5000H to 5002H the same as they were in the first example. The last thing to change will be the op-code. We'll change that to LDDR. This will repeat the LDD command until the contents of BC are 00H.

Here are the results.

Location	Contents	Location	Contents
3C00H	41H	5000H	41H
3C01H	42H	5001H	42H
3C02H	43H	5002H	43H
3C03H	20H		

The contents of BC will be 00H.
The contents of HL will be 4FFFH.
The contents of DE will be 3BFFH.

Note that the same thing as the LDIR command was accomplished but the contents of all the register pairs were decremented.

SEARCHES

Since we have mastered the first two parts of this chapter, we will look at the SEARCH group. In machine language we SEARCH for things by comparing two things. This is done by comparing a standard to something else. The something else could be data, or a value that we have preset somewhere in the program. Then, having found or not found a true or exact comparison, some action occurs.

For example, if I give you a big bowl that contains every type of nut in the world and tell you to find a Brazil nut in the bowl, then stand up, you may ask me, "what's a Brazil nut?"

To save a lot of hassle trying to explain it to you, I'll put a Brazil nut in your left hand, and tell you to find one like it in the bowl then stand up. If you go through the entire bowl and don't find one, raise your hand.

In doing this you will compare all the nuts in the bowl to the one in your left hand, and then respond accordingly when you do or don't find a match.

This is called SEARCHing by comparison, and it is how the computer does it.

I know the computer can't raise its hand or stand up. For this reason, we tell it to set what is called a CONDITION FLAG.

Setting a CONDITION FLAG means setting the value of a byte to one or zero, depending on the condition.

I won't get technical about this, but I will say that the condition will be stored in the F register, and the A register will be used to hold the nut, or the value (standard) we want to look for.

For this reason, we cannot disturb the AF register pairs or A or F registers once we begin the search.

FLAGS

Table 9-1 is a list of the flags and what they do. I'll explain each flag so we will know what we are doing when we are using the search procedure.

The carry flag C tells the computer that the value was too large for that column (as in adding and carrying) or that we had to borrow (as in subtraction). That's the most common use for the C flag (addition and subtraction).

The add / subtract flag N is used to determine if the command calls for an add function, or a subtract function. We saw one example of this in the LDI and LDD instructions. Here we had to add or subtract from the contents of a register pair. Just for the record, the N flag will be set to 0 for all add functions, and set to 1 for all subtract functions.

The parity / overflow flag P/V flag is set when an overflow condition results from an add or subtract routine. An overflow will never occur when you add two values with unlike signs (example: +100 added to −500). Overflow can occur when adding values with like signs, (ex +100 added to +500 or −100 added to −500). The opposite is true when using the subtraction function. Overflow can occur when subtracting unlike signs, and will never occur when subtracting like signs.

The half carry flag, or the H flag is primarily used to adjust the decimal point during add and subtract functions.

Table 9-1. Introduction to Flags.

FLAG	USE
C	carry flag
N	add / subtract flag
P/V	parity / overflow flag
H	half carry flag
Z	zero flag
S	sign flag

The zero, or Z flag tells us what the status of the accumulator is. If the value in the accumulator is zero, the Z flag is set to 1. If the value is not zero, it is set to 0.

The last flag is the sign flag or the S flag. This flag tells the computer whether the contents of the accumulator is a positive or a negative number. If the number is positive, the value of the S flag will be zero, if it is negative, the value of the S flag will be one.

COMPARE COMMANDS

Now let's look at some COMPARE commands.

The first one in the SEARCH group is the CPI command. It will look like this:

CPI

The computer will know what to do so we don't need an operand. The command tells the computer to COMPARE the value stored in the location pointed to by the HL register pair with the value in the accumulator. In case of a true comparison, a flag is set in the F register, and the contents of the HL register pair is incremented. At the same time, the contents of the BC register pair is decremented.

Let's run that by again. Let's say that the contents of the HL register pair is 3C01H, and the contents of location 3C01H is 20H. Also let's say that the contents of the A register is 20H. Finally, imagine that the contents of the BC register pair is 05H.

Now, after the command

CPI ;

the computer has checked the contents of 3C01H, (the location stored in the HL register pair) with the contents of the A register. It found that they matched because when it subtracted the contents of 3C01H from the contents of the A register the result was zero as both were 20H. Therefore the S flag was reset, and the Z flag was set. It then incremented the HL register pair, and decremented the contents of the BC register pair.

The following conditions now exist.

The contents of the BC register pair are 04H.
The contents of the HL register pair are 3C02H.
The contents of location 3C01H is still 20H.
The contents of the A register is still 20H.
The Z flag is set.
The S flag is reset.

Now we can tell the computer what to do if the Z flag is set. But suppose that the value in the A register was 21H, and everything else was the same? Here's what that would look like.

The contents of the BC register pair are 05H.
The contents of the HL register pair are 3C01H.
The contents of location 3C01H is 20H.
The contents of the A register is 21H.
The Z flag is not set.
The S flag is not set, but would have been if the A register contained 1FH.

This process can be repeated automatically but not with this instruction. We have to use the CPIR instruction to do that.

Let's use the same information that we used in the last example, and change the op-code to CPIR. The machine will test memory locations until one of the following two things happen.

1. A true comparison is found.
2. The contents of the BC register pair has been decremented to zero.

First, if a true comparison is found, the computer will act as it did when it found a true comparison in the CPI instruction. However, if no true comparison is found the HL register pair will be incremented, and the BC register pair will be decremented.

One other interesting thing happens. The Program Counter (PC) will be decremented by two, since the CPIR instruction is a two-byte instruction. This will cause the command to be repeated. This will continue until the contents of the BC register pair has been decremented to ZERO.

But what if the contents of the BC register pair was zero at the start of the instruction? In this case the machine will cycle through 64K bytes unless it finds a true comparison. If it finds no true comparison, it will then proceed to the next instruction, and the Z flag will not be set.

The next two commands are exactly like the first two but with one small change. Instead of the contents of the HL register pair being incremented, it is decremented.

Let's look at the CPD command, and COMPARE it to the CPI command. To do this we will use the same conditions that we used for the CPI command. The results will be the same with the exception that instead of the contents of the HL register pair being incremented, they will be decremented. The important things to remember are;

1. The contents of the HL register pair are decremented.
2. The COMPARE function is the same.

The last op-code in this group, CPDR, is very similar to the CPIR op-code. Again, the major difference is that the contents of the HL register pair are decremented instead of incremented. The function and rules are the same in both the CPIR and CPDR commands. However, there is one thing that is common to both commands that we have overlooked up to now. After each data comparison has been made, interrupts will be recognized. ***Interrupts cause the computer to stop doing certain functions due to certain conditions.***

What is an interrupt? We won't get to that in this book as it is for advanced use only. Just keep in mind that interrupts will be recognized.

QUIZ

1. ________ tells the computer to exchange the contents of the BC register pair with its primed counterpart and at the same time to exchange the contents of the DE and HL register pairs with their primed counter parts.
2. ________ is the instruction to exchange the AF register pair with the AF′ register pair.
3. The ______ instruction transfers a byte of data from the address pointed to by the HL register pair to the address pointed to by the DE register pair. It then increments the DE and HL register pairs.
4. The ________ instruction performs the same action as the command in question 3 but the command is repeated.
5. The ________ instruction is the same as the instruction in question 3 but the HL and DE register pairs are decremented.
6. The ________ instruction is the same as the instruction in question 5 but the instruction is repeated.
7. CP means ________.
8. The ________ instruction tells the computer to compare the value in the A register with the value in the location pointed to by the HL register pair. In case of a true comparison, a flag is set in the F register, and the contents of the HL register pair is incremented. At the same time the BC register pair is decremented.
9. The ________ instruction is the same as the instruction in question 8 except that the contents of the location pointed to by the HL register pair are decremented.
10. ________ is the same as question 8 but the command is repeated.
11. ________ is the same as question 9 but the command is repeated.
12. List the 6 flags and tell their uses.

ANSWERS

1. EXX
2. EX
3. LDI
4. LDIR
5. LDD
6. LDDR
7. COMPARE
8. CPI
9. CPD
10. CPIR
11. CPDR
12. C carry
    N add/subtract
    P/V parity/overflow
    H half carry
    Z zero
    S sign

Chapter 10
The 8-Bit Arithmetic Group

In machine language, only two arithmetic functions are permitted. These are add and subtract. Multiplication and division are done by repetitive addition and repetitive subtraction.

REPETITIVE ADDITION AND SUBTRACTION

How can you multiply by adding, and divide by subtracting? Take out a piece of paper and write down the number 3 ten times in a column. Add the column. The answer was 30. Try it again using any number. The answer still comes out the same as it would have if you multiplied the number by the number of times it appeared in the column. You have just multiplied by repetitive addition.

Now, let's divide using subtraction. This time write down the number 30, and subtract 3 from it. You'll get 27. Subtract 3 from the 27, and continue the process until you have subtracted five times.

30−3=27   27−3=24   24−3=21   21−3=18   18−3=15

Get the picture? Five is half of 10. Ten times 3 is 30. Half of 30 is 15. Here again, you have just divided by repetitive subtraction.

The important thing to remember is that the A register (the accumulator) carries the number to be added or subtracted.

ADD COMMANDS

There are five different ADD commands. The first one tells the computer to ADD the contents of a register to the A register. The register can be the A, B, C, D, E, H, or L register. Note the absence of the F register. This one will contain the flag condition, and for that reason it cannot be used.

Let's see what happens if we ADD the contents of the H register to the A register. Suppose the H register contains the value 10H and the A register contains the value 05H. Then after the command

```
ADD     A,H
```

The H register will still contain 10H, but the A register will now contain 15H,or the sum of the two registers. What about the condition of the flags? Let's examine them.

The S FLAG will be RESET.
The Z FLAG will be RESET.
The H FLAG will be RESET.
The P/V FLAG will be RESET.
The N FLAG will be RESET.
The C FLAG will be RESET.

You take the flags and find out why the conditions are what they are. Hint—they would be different if the numbers were 10 and 10.

Answer—The H flag will be set due to the carry.

To add, use this command.

```
ADD     A,N
```

In this instruction, the number represented by the N is added to the contents of the accumulator. Since this is an 8-bit load, the number N cannot exceed 255 or FFH.

Now for an example. If the contents of the accumulator is 10H, and we replace the N with 15H, then after the instruction

```
ADD     A,15H
```

Register	Contents	Value Added	New Contents
A	10H	15H	25H

The accumulator will contain 25H. We could also add a decimal number to the accumulator. Let's substitute the 15H for it's decimal equivalent 21.

ADD A,21

Note that the 21 was not followed by the letter H. The computer will treat this number as a decimal and add it to the contents of the accumulator after it converts it to a hex number (21 decimal = 15H).

What about the flags? They follow the same rules as they did in the last example. They also follow the same rules for the entire 8-bit arithmetic group.

Now let's ADD the contents of a memory location to the A register. The command looks like this:

ADD A,(HL)

If the contents of the A register is 10, and the HL register pair contains 4000H, and location 4000H contains 15H, then after this instruction, the results are as follows. Table 10-2.

Before

Register	Register Pair	Location
A	HL	4000H
10H	4000H	15H

After

Register	Register Pair	Location
A	HL	4000H
25H	4000H	15H

The HL register pair will contain 4000H.
The contents of location 4000H will be 15H.
The A register will contain 25H.

The same rules hold true for the last two ADD commands. These are:

```
ADD     A,(IX+D)
ADD     A,(IY+D)
```

Remember that the D is the displacement. By the way, if no

displacement is given, the computer will look at the address contained in the IX or IY register pair. Ex;

ADD A,(IX)
ADD A,(IX+5)

If the contents of the IX register pair is 4000H, then in the first instruction, the contents of location 4000H is ADDed to the contents of the A register. However, in the second instruction, the contents of location 4005H (4000H + 5) is ADDed to the A register.

SPECIAL ADD

So much for the routine ADD instructions. Now, we have one more special ADD instruction. This is the ADC instruction.

The ADC instruction means ADD with CARRY. In other words, ADD the contents of the register, memory location, or ADD the number to the A register and CARRY the excess, just as you did in fourth grade.

If the A register contains 16H, and the carry flag is set, and we ADD 10H to it, this is what will happen:

ADC A,10H
ADC C flag is set

Register	Contents	Value Added	New Contents
A	16H	10H	27H

The A register will then contain 27H. I know that 10H and 16H added together are 26H, but remember this is ADD with CARRY, and the carry flag was set. We caught that loose one floating around didn't we.

SUBTRACTION COMMANDS

Now for subtraction. The SUB is the same as the ADD.

SUB A,H

If the A register contains 10H, and the H register contains 05H, then after this instruction is executed, the contents of the A register will be 5H.

The same variations of the SUB command exist as they did for the ADD command. However, you may want to pay attention to the sign flag as it may be negative in some cases.

Here's a little exercise for you. Write down the flag conditions for the example above. Then re-write them only under the following conditions:

The contents of the A register are 05H.

The contents of the H register is 10H.

Answer: The N flag will be set.
The S flag will be set.

Notice the difference. If you subtract 16 from 5 you'll get a negative 11.

The last SUBTRACT command is the SBC or SUBTRACT with CARRY (or in this case borrow) command. This command is similar to the ADC command, except that it is a subtract command. It also follows the standard SUBTRACT rules.

Let's suppose that the contents of the A register is 16H, and the carry flag is set. Let's also say that we want to SUBTRACT 05H from the A register. The command will look like this:

```
SBC     A,05H
```

The result will be that the A register will contain 10H. Again, note that the carry flag was set, which in this case caused a borrowing condition to occur. That was easy enough.

LOGICAL AND

Now, let's try a difficult one, the AND command. This is a LOGICAL AND operation in which a bit-by-bit ADD is performed. "A bit-by-bit ADD of what, you ask?" There are eleven possible combinations for this command. They are:

AND	R (where R is any of the B, C, D, E, H, L, or A registers.
AND	N (where N is any number up to FFH)
AND	(HL) (where HL points to a location)
AND	(IX+D)
AND	(IY+D)

When the computer encounters an AND command, it will perform a binary or analogous ADD. The results will be stored in the accumulator (A) register. Here is an example.

If the contents of the A register is C3H, this means that the binary value stored in the A register is 11000011. If at the same time the H register contains 7BH then the B register contains the binary number 01111011. When the computer encounters

AND B

this is the way it will ADD the registers:

	B	01111011
	A	11000011
	---	-----
Total	A	01000011 or 43H.

Remember that in a logical binary ADD,

$0 + 0 = 0$
$1 + 1 = 1$
$1 + 0 = 0$

This is how we got the 43H.

MASKING

The most common use for the AND is as a mask. A mask is used to cover up something that you don't want acted upon. In this case we don't want something to be stored in the A register.

Let's look at an example. The hex code for the keyboard numbers 0 through 9 are 30H through 39H. Suppose you want to store the digit in the A register and not the hex value. You could do this by SUBTRACTing 30H from the number, but it would be easier to mask out the three. If the A register contains 30H, and we mask out the three using the instruction

AND 0FH

then only the last four bits of the byte will fall through during the ADD function. This is because 0FH is 00001111 in binary; 30H is 11110000. This, when ADDED, produces 00000000 in binary, or the 0 that we wanted.

OR COMMANDS

The next command is the OR command. This command uses a *true* binary ADD to perform the analogous ADD function. Unlike the last binary ADD that we discussed, the

LOGICAL ADD, where the only way the answer could be a one was if the two numbers added together were both one, the true binary ADD looks like this:

1 + 1 = 1
1 + 0 = 1
0 + 0 = 0

Under this type of addition, if we say that the A register contains 48H (01001000), and the H register contains 12H (00010010), we get 5AH (01011010) when we perform the OR operation. Let's see how that works.

```
OR    H
A     48H    01001000
H     12H    00010010
---   ---    -------
A     5AH    01011010
```

Note that in this case if we had added 12H and 48H, we would have come up with 5AH anyway. The OR command can be performed in any of the following ways.

1. It can be used with any of the following registers; B, C, D, E, H, L, and A.
2. It can be used to ADD numbers up to FFH.
3. It can be used to ADD the contents of a location specified by the HL register pair. (OR (HL))
4. It can be used with the IX and IY register pairs (OR (IX+D) OR (IY+D)).

XOR

There is also a special OR command that is referred to as the EXCLUSIVE OR or the XOR command. This command can also be used in the same manner as the AND and OR commands as far as the operands are concerned. However since it is a special or exclusive command, it does have a special use, which is to zero the accumulator. If we execute the command

XOR A

the contents of the accumulator will be zero after the instruction is executed.

Now that you have learned some of the hard stuff, let's review a little and learn some more easy things.

8-BIT COMPARE

In the last chapter we learned some COMPARE commands, that we used in a SEARCH group. Let's look at a simple and very common COMPARE. In this COMPARE we will only compare 8 bits. By the way, this is the compare that you will probably use often. Here it is and here are the ways it can be used.

CP B

The contents of the B register or any of the C, D, E, H, L, or A registers are compared with the contents of the A register. Then a flag is set in the F register, and the program continues to the next instruction. The next instruction usually tells the computer what to do if the condition of the F register meets certain specifications defined by the program line.

The other possible combinations are:

CP N

Where N is a number not over FFH.

CP (HL)

Compare with the contents of the address specified by the HL register pair.

CP (IX+D)

Compare with the address pointed to by the IX register pair plus the displacement D.

CP (IY+D)

Same as the (IX+D).

THE INCREMENT COMMAND

Easy? Well, here's an easier one.

INC R.

Third command INCREMENTs a register, R, where R is any of the A, B, C, D, E, H, or L registers. For example, if the H register contains 05H, after the command

INC H

the H register will contain 06H. Also the F register will carry flag showing the condition caused by the INC instruction.

The INC command can also be used to increment the contents. If the HL, IX+D, or IY+D register pairs look like this:

```
INC     (HL)
INC     (IX+D)
INC     (IY+D)
```

here again the appropriate flags will be set.

THE DECREMENT COMMAND

The last command in this group is the DEC or DECREMENT command. If you will remember, we discussed decrement in the last chapter. It means subtract.

The DEC command can be performed on any of the B, C, D, E, H, L, or A registers. It can also be performed on the contents of the HL register pair, (HL), and on the contents of the IX+D and IY+D register pairs (IX+D) and (IY+D).

When the DEC command is encountered, the value stored in the register or memory location is decreased by one. For example, if the B register contains 05H, after the command

```
DEC     B
```

the B register will contain 04H.

As in the INC command, the F register will contain the flags pertaining to the register status after this command has been executed. These status conditions can range from the S flag being set to the P/V flag being set.

QUIZ

1. Show how to add the number 15H to the contents of the A register.
2. What would the contents of the A register be in question 1 if the A register contained 0AH before the ADD?
3. If the A register contains FFH, and the H register contains 10H, show the command to subtract the contents of the H register from the A register.
4. Using the information in question 3, show the before and after contents of the A and H registers.
5. What does ADC mean?
6. What does SBC mean?
7. When the computer encounters the ________ command, it will perform a binary or analogous add.
8. The ________ instruction uses a true binary add to perform the analogous add.
9. Show how to compare the value in the A register to the contents of the HL register pair.
10. What does DEC mean?
11. What does INC mean?
12. Show how to add 1 to the contents of the HL register pair using the INC command.
13. Using the DEC instruction, subtract 1 from the contents of the HL register pair.

ANSWERS

1. ADD A,H
2. 1FH
3. SUB A,H
4. | Register | A | H |
   | --- | --- | --- |
   | Before | FFH | 10H |
   | After | EFH | 10H |
5. ADD with CARRY
6. SUBTRACT with CARRY (OR BORROW)
7. AND
8. OR
9. CP (HL)
10. decrement
11. increment
12. INC (HL)
13. DEC (HL)

Chapter 11
General-Purpose Arithmetic and CPU Control Groups

Let's proceed to the first command in this group, the DAA command.

THE DAA COMMAND

The DAA command adjusts the accumulator for the BCD addition and subtraction operations. BCD stands for binary coded decimal.

Suppose we wanted to add 15 decimal and 27 decimal. We want the answer to be in hex because the computer understands hex. Let's see what happens when we add the two numbers.

$$15 + 27 = 42$$

Look at the binary numbers:

Dec	Binary	Dec	Binary
1	0001	5	0101
2	0010	7	0111
—	——	—	——
3	0011	C	1100

That gave us 3C for an answer, but we wanted 42. What happened?

The computer is working with hex, and we are working with decimal. However, the computer recognizes binary for both numbering systems. To adjust for this we use the DAA instruction. It appears with no operand.

The DAA instruction automatically adds the proper conversion to the answer. Here's how.

Hex	Binary	Hex	Binary
3	0011	C	1100
	0000		0110
4	0100	2	0010

Don't worry about the values that are added. We used this as an example. The important thing to remember is that the DAA instruction automatically makes the adjustment.

CPL COMMAND

Suppose that you wanted to invert the contents of the A register. We have a command to do that too.

CPL

When the computer encounters this instruction, it inverts the contents of the A register in a 1's complement. Here's an example.

Bit No.	1	2	3	4	5	6	7	8
A REG. before	1	0	1	1	0	1	0	0
A REG. after CPL	0	1	0	0	1	0	1	1

The values of the first four bits of the A register are in the same order, but are in the last four bits of the A register, and the last four are now in the first four. The values in bits 1 and 5 are reversed, the values in bits 2 and 6 are reversed, the values in bits 3 and 7 are reversed, and the values in bits 4 and 8 are reversed.

THE NEG COMMAND

Another command you may not need for a while is the NEG command. When this instruction is encountered, the contents of the A register are negated in 2's complement. This is the same as subtracting the contents of the accumulator from zero. If the register contained +10, the NEG instruction would cause the A register to contain a – 10. Let's look at an example of this command.

Bit No.	1	2	3	4	5	6	7	8
A REG. before NEG	1	0	0	1	1	0	0	0
A REG. after NEG	0	1	1	0	1	0	0	0

Note that the binary values in the first four bits are reversed from what they were before the NEG command.

CCF AND SCF

Up until now we haven't talked much about the F register. The next two instructions, CCF and SCF, will deal strictly with the F register.

The CCF instruction has no operand and inverts the CARRY FLAG in the F register.

This instruction, SCF sets the carry flag in the F register. The three flags affected will be the H flag, which will be reset; the N flag, which will be reset; and the CARRY flag, which will be set.

THE NOP COMMAND

The next instruction is called a no-op or NOP. It is used mostly in machine language but can also be used in assembly language. When the computer encounters a NOP, it performs no operation. It simply passes over the instruction and goes to the next one.

If this is true, then why would it be used in machine language? In machine language, you will most likely be using T-BUG to program the machine. If you wanted to reserve an area inside the program, a buffer, you would fill this area with no-ops. The machine code for a NOP is 00 so you would have an area filled with 0s, and this would assure you that you don't have any value hung up in the area.

The next six instructions in this section are used only by the most advanced programmers. They are HALT, DI, EI, IM 0, IM 1, and IM 2. We will not discuss these because we don't want to lose or confuse you. However, after you have mastered this language and have been using it for sometime, I suggest that you read some more advanced books that deal with these instructions.

QUIZ

1. What is the CPU?
2. What is meant by BCD?
3. What command adjusts the accumulator for BCD and subtract?
4. What instruction adjusts decimal to hex?
5. What is the name given to the instruction that inverts the contents of the A register?
6. The ____ instruction subtracts the contents of the A
7. The ________ instruction inverts the carry flag in the F register.
8. __________ can be used to reserve space in a program.

ANSWERS

1. central processing unit
2. binary coded decimal
3. DAA
4. DAA
5. CPL
6. NEG
7. CCF
8. no-op or NOP

Chapter 12

The 16-Bit Arithmetic Group

In this chapter we will discuss the 16-bit ADD, SUBTRACT, INCREMENT, and DECREMENT commands. These are very similar to the 8-bit commands. The main difference is that 8-bit uses single registers, whereas 16-bit uses register pairs.

16-BIT ADDS

The first one is

```
ADD     HL,SS
```

where SS is any of the BC, DE, HL, or SP register pairs. For example, if the HL register contains the number 2121H, and the DE register pair contains 4534H, then after the command

```
ADD     HL,DE
```

You will see the following results.

Before

Reg. Pair	Contents	Reg. Pair	Contents
HL	2121H	DE	4534H

After

Reg. Pair	Contents	Reg. Pair	Contents
HL	6655H	DE	4534H

The contents of the HL register pair will be 6655H. This is because the ADD of 2121H and 4534H took place. You must be careful with this command or you may do something disastrous. You may ADD something that you don't want.

Don't forget, the contents of the register pairs are added together. If you have a memory location stored in one of these register pairs, and you don't move it somewhere (store it in a buffer, PUSH it to the top of the stack, or load it into another register pair), you will end up adding a number to the contents of a register pair that, instead of having another number in it, has a memory location in it. Here's an example.

Let's say the DE register pair is pointing to 3C00H, the HL register pair contains 4000H, and location 3C00H contains 41H. If you forgot to PUSH DE and reload it with the value that you wanted when you execute the instruction,

```
ADD     HL,DE
```

you will cause the contents of HL to be 7C00H. The contents of DE will remain the same, and the contents of 3C00H will still be 41H. The problem will be that the value in the HL register pair will not be what you wanted.

An error like this could take hours to find, so be careful.

The next command is the ADC command. The definition of the ADC command is Add with Carry. This command is executed in the same manner as the ADD command but in this case the carry flag in the F register is added to the contents of HL and the result is stored in the HL register pair.

Here's an example. Given the contents of the HL register pair as 5437H, the contents of the DE register pair as 2222H, and the carry flag in the F register as set, the command

```
ADC     HL,DE
```

would cause the contents of the HL register pair to be 765AH. If we added 5437H to 2222H, we would get 7659H. But since the carry flag in the F register was set, and we used the ADC command, the extra 1H was added to 7659H producing 765AH.

SBC

The same is true in the SBC command (Subtract with Carry). In the SCB HL,RR command the RR stands for any of the BC, DE, HL, or SP register pairs. A good example of this command would be the following.

Given the contents of the HL register pair as 6666H, the contents of the DE register pair as 2222H, and the C flag in the F register as set. Under these conditions, execution of

SBC HL,DE

would produce the following: The contents of the DE register pair would still be 2222H. The contents of the HL register pair would be 4443H. This is because the carry flag in the F register was set, and the SBC (Subtract with Carry command) was executed.

MORE ADDS

The next instruction is the ADD IX,PP command. In this instruction, PP is any of the following register pairs:

BC, DE, IX, or SP.

Although it is carried out in the same manner as the ADD HL,RR instruction and produces exactly the same type of answer, through exactly the same type of an ADD routine, the HL register pair cannot be used in this instruction. The key to remembering this command is that whatever is added to the IX register pair cannot be in the HL register pair.

The last ADD instruction is ADD IY,RR. In this instruction, RR is either the BC, DE, IY, or SP register pairs. Again, notice the absence of the HL register pair in this instruction. ADD IY,RR is just like the ADD HL,RR instruction, and produces exactly the same type of answer, through exactly the same type of an ADD routine, but the HL register pair cannot be used in this instruction. The key to remembering this one is that whatever is added to the IY register pair cannot be in the HL or IX register pairs.

INC AND DEC

The last two commands in this group are INC and DEC. These functions can be performed on any of the HL, DE, BC, SP, IX, or IY register pairs. As in the increment and decrement instructions for the 8-bit arithmetic group, the contents of the register pairs are either incremented or decremented by one.

For example, if the contents of the DE register pair is 3C01H, then executing

```
INC     DE
```

would result in the DE register pair containing 3C02H. By the same token, executing

```
DEC     DE
```

would result in the DE register pair containing 3C00H.

QUIZ

1. The main difference between the 8-bit arithmetic group and the 16-bit arithmetic group is that the 8-bit group uses __________ while the 16-bit uses __________.
2. Give the before and after for these conditions. ADD HL,DE given HL contains 1315H and DE contains 3F8EH.
3. Tell what the difference is between the following instructions.

```
A. LD    A,(HL)
B. LD    DE,(HL)
C. LD    DE,HL
```

ANSWERS

1. registers   register pairs
2. register pair HL   DE
3. A. load the A register with the contents of the HL register pair. This is an 8-bit load.

   B. load the DE register pair with the contents of the HL register pair. This is a 16-bit load.

   C. load DE with HL. This is a 16-bit load.

Chapter 13
The Rotate and Shift Group

This chapter may be a little difficult, but it is extremely important. As a machine-language programmer, there will be various routines that you will want to perform. The material in this chapter will help you do many intricate routines with ease.

ROTATE

Let's get down to business. The first part of this group is the ROTATE section. You will soon learn what a ROTATE is, and what happens when a ROTATE is executed. But, first let me give you a primary rule of thumb.

Generally, when you ROTATE left, you will be performing a multiply by two. When you ROTATE right you will be performing a division routine.

Earlier, I said that in machine language we can't multiply and divide. We have to use repetitive adds and subtracts. That was and is and will always be true. A ROTATE is just another way to accomplish this.

Let's look at the first ROTATE. It's RLCA (Rotate Left with Carry Arithmetic). This instruction has no operand as the operand is understood.

When the computer encounters this instruction, it automatically moves the contents of each bit, starting with bit 0 to the next bit to the left. The contents of the last bit are moved into the carry flag in the F register and the first bit in the byte. That's why we call it Rotate Left with Carry Arithmetic. Here's an example:

Condition of byte before RLCA

Bit No.	7	6	5	4	3	2	1	0
Contents	1	0	0	0	1	0	0	0

Condition of byte after RLCA

Bit No.	C	7	6	5	4	3	2	1	0
Contents	1	0	0	0	1	0	0	0	1

Notice how the ROTATE was performed. Now look at the decimal value of the number before and after. I'll leave this up to you, but you should be able to see the change in value and guess what would happen if we repeated the instruction several times.

Decimal before 72

Decimal after 1st RLCA 144 (17 in this byte and 127 in the next byte)

Now let's look at the RLA (Rotate Left Arithmetic) instruction. Here we see that the contents of each bit is ROTATE left into the next register just as in the RLCA instruction.

There is one catch. The contents of the last bit are moved into the carry flag but are not moved into the first bit as well. Instead, the previous contents of the carry flag are moved into the first bit.

Before

Bit No.	C	7	6	5	4	3	2	1	0
Contents	1	0	1	1	1	0	1	1	0

After

Bit No.	C	7	6	5	4	3	2	1	0
Contents	0	1	1	1	0	1	1	0	1

The next two instructions are like the first two except we are going to ROTATE right. The first one is ROTATE Right with Carry Arithmetic or RRCA.

As you will see from the example, the same thing will happen to the byte as it did in the RLCA command with the exception that the ROTATE will be to the RIGHT.

Before

Bit No.	7	6	5	4	3	2	1	0	
Contents	0	0	0	1	0	0	1	0	

After the RRCA command

Bit No.	7	6	5	4	3	2	1	0	
Contents	0	0	0	0	1	0	0	1	0

Before going on to the next instruction, write down these two examples in binary and convert them to decimal.

decimal before	18
decimal after 1st RRCA	9

Note the change in the value that the RRCA command made.

The next instruction is the Rotate Right Arithmetic or RRA command. This command is exactly like the RLA command but again the ROTATE is to the right. This example should show you exactly what happens.

Before RRA

Bit No.	7	6	5	4	3	2	1	0	C
Condition	1	1	1	0	0	0	0	1	0

After the RRA command

Bit No.	7	6	5	4	3	2	1	0	C
Condition	0	1	1	1	0	0	0	0	1

Note that the previous contents of the carry flag are copied into bit 7, and that the previous contents of bit 0 are copied into the carry flag.

Here, again, I want you to copy the binary numbers down and convert them to decimal. I want you to become familiar with what has happened.

The next four instructions deal with the Rotate Left with Carry command.

In this command, the contents of each bit in a byte are ROTATE left to the next bit. The contents of bit 7 are moved to the carry flag and also into bit 0.

These are the four possible combinations of the RLC command

```
RLC    R
RLC    (HL)
RLC    (IX+D)
RLC    (IY+D)
```

In these instructions, the R represents any of the B, C, D, E, H, L, or A registers. The D in the IX+D and IY+D represents the displacement just as it has in previous chapters.

These instructions are the same as the RLC instruction, with the same things happening to the contents of the register R, or the contents of the memory location addressed by the HL register pair, or the IX or IY register pairs. These are the various ways that the RLC instruction can be used.

The next instruction is the RL instruction. This instruction ROTATE the contents of each bit left to the next bit. Bit 7 is moved into the carry flag, and the contents of the carry flag are moved into bit 0. Following the various combinations allowed with this instruction.

```
RL    B
RL    C
RL    D
RL    E
RL    H
RL    L
RL    A
RL    (HL)
RL    (IX+D)
RL    (IY+D)
```

Before RL

Bit No.	C	7	6	5	4	3	2	1	0
Condition	0	1	0	0	0	1	1	1	1

After the RL command

Bit No.	C	7	6	5	4	3	2	1	0
Condition	1	0	0	0	1	1	1	1	0

As you can see in Table 13-1, this instruction is used to ROTATE left the contents of a register, the contents of the HL register pair, or the contents of the IX or IY register pairs.

The next instruction is the Rotate Right with Carry instruction or RRC. This instruction is exactly like the RLC instruction except the rotate is done to the right. The various possible instruction combinations are the same as the RLC command, but again the ROTATE is made to the right.

The last ROTATE instruction is the Rotate Right or RR instruction. Here again, we find that this instruction is exactly the same as the RL instruction and is used with the same operands. However, the difference is that the ROTATE is to the right and not the left.

SHIFT

The next set of instructions are the SHIFT instructions. Unlike a ROTATE, a SHIFT causes the first bit on the side that you start the SHIFT to be reset, and the value of the last bit is lost.

The first SHIFT that we will be looking at is the Shift Left Arithmetic or SLA. The SLA command can be executed on any of the B, C, D, E, H, L, or A registers. It also can be executed on the contents of the HL, IX+D, or IY+D register pairs. Let's see what happens when this instruction is executed.

If the contents of the A register are:

Bit No.	7	6	5	4	3	2	1	0
Contents	0	0	0	0	1	1	1	1

then after the execution of

SLA A

the contents of the A register will be

Bit No.	C	7	6	5	4	3	2	1	0
Contents	0	0	0	0	1	1	1	1	0

Notice that the contents of BIT 7 were SHIFTed to the carry flag in the F register, and that bit 0 was reset. Write down the above numbers in binary and convert them to decimal. After you have done that note their relationship.

decimal before	15
decimal after 1st SLA	30

The next instruction is the Shift Right Arithmetic or SRA instruction. In this instruction everything is the same as the SLA instruction except the fact that the SHIFT is to the right, and the previous contents of bit 7 are unchanged. Here's an example:

Before SRA

Bit No.	7	6	5	4	3	2	1	0	
Contents	0	0	1	1	1	0	0	0	

After SRA

Bit No.	7	6	5	4	3	2	1	0	C
Contents	0	1	0	1	1	1	0	0	0

decimal before 56
decimal after 1st RLCA 28

QUIZ

1. When we use a __________ we will be multiplying by 2.
2. When we use a __________ we will be dividing by 2.
3. Tell what the difference is between the following instructions.

A	RLC	E	RRCA
B	RL	F	RRA
C	RLCA	G	SLA
D	RLA	H	SRA

ANSWERS

1. ROTATE left
2. ROTATE right
3. A. Rotate Left with Carry
   B. Rotate Left
   C. Rotate Left with Carry Arithmetic
   D. Rotate Left Arithmetic
   E. Rotate Right with Carry Arithmetic
   F. Rotate Right Arithmetic
   G. Shift Left Arithmetic
   H. Shift Right Arithmetic

Chapter 14

Bit Set, Reset, and Test Group

In this chapter, we will learn some very interesting things about bits. For example, you can actually test any bit of any register to see if it's a 1 or a 0. "Why would I want to do that?" you ask. Well, later, you will learn how to go to different places in your programs. It might be nice to be able to test the condition of a bit and, depending on the condition of that bit, go to another routine.

Another thing that you will learn in this chapter is how to change the value of just one bit in a byte. This is useful if you need to set the value of a test bit if a certain condition was met, and then go to your subroutine. If you did this, the condition would remain the same until you changed it back. Some useful examples of this would be in game and business programs.

In game programs you could create a condition that would tell you if a move was legal or if a square had been played. You could also use these functions to keep score.

In business, for example, if you needed to show if an account were open or closed, you could use this function. It could also be used to show inventory status.

BIT

Let's look at the first instruction in this group. It is BIT.

BIT B,R

Where B is any bit from 0 through 7, and R is any of the B, C, D, E, H, L, or A registers. R may also denote the contents of the address specified by the HL, IX+D or IY+D register pairs.

When the BIT command is performed, the Z flag in the F register will contain the complement of the bit that was tested.

If the bit tested was one, then the Z flag would be zero. On the other hand, if the bit tested was a zero, then the Z flag in the F register would be one. That's simple enough.

Now let's look at an example of the instruction. If the Z flag in the F register is zero, and bit five in the H register is zero, then when we execute

BIT 5,H

the Z flag in the F register will be 1, and bit five in the H register will still be zero, as follows:

Before BIT 5,H

Bit No.	7	6	5	4	3	2	1	0	Z
Condition	1	1	0	0	0	0	0	1	0

After BIT 5,H

Bit No.	7	6	5	4	3	2	1	0	Z
Condition	1	1	0	0	0	0	0	1	1

Later we will find out how setting the Z flag would be of use to us. But at this time the important thing is to see and understand how it is done.

SET

The next instruction is the SET instruction. It looks like this:

SET B,R

Just as in the BIT instruction, the B stands for the bit number, and the R stands for the register or register pairs. The bit can be any one from 0 to seven, and the register can be any of the B, C, D, E, H, L, or A registers. Also the R can signify the contents of the memory location addressed by the HL, IX+D or IY+D register pairs.

The SET instruction causes the bit specified to be SET in the register or location specified. By setting we mean that the value of the bit is SET to one.

For example, if bit three of the L register is zero then after the execution of

SET 3,L

the contents of bit 3 in the L register will be one, as follows:

Before SET 3,L

Bit No.	7 6 5 4 3 2 1 0 Z
Condition	1 1 1 0 0 0 0 1 0

After SET 3,L

Bit No.	7 6 5 4 3 2 1 0 Z
Condition	1 1 1 0 1 0 0 1 1

This will be useful in setting a standard value to test the BIT instruction. Even though it is not good programming practice to jump back and forth, let's see what would happen if we did a BIT 3,L on the example that we used in the SET instruction.

BIT 3,L

Bit No.	7 6 5 4 3 2 1 0 Z
Condition	1 1 1 0 0 0 0 1 0

If we did it before we did the SET instruction the Z flag would be reset. However, after the SET instruction, the Z flag would be SET, as follows:

After the SET command

Bit No.	7 6 5 4 3 2 1 0 Z
Condition	1 1 1 0 1 0 0 1 1

If you don't see how and why, read the BIT and SET instructions again.

Now, if we don't want bit three in the L register set, we can RESET it by using the RES COMMAND, which looks like this:

RES B,R

Where R is any of the B, C, D, E, H, L, or A registers. As in the SET instruction, R could also mean the contents of the memory location specified by the contents of the H1, IX+D, or IY+D register pairs. Performing the command:

RES 3,L

would cause bit three in the L register to contain a zero. If we then executed

BIT 3,L

the Z flag in the F register would be RESET.

QUIZ

1. Show how to test the 5th bit in the L register.
2. Show how to set the 1st bit in the A register.
3. How would you change the 7th bit in the D register if it was 1?

ANSWERS

1. BIT 5,L
2. SET 1,A
3. RES 7,D

Chapter 15
The Jump Group

This is the group that you've been waiting for. It will allow you to go places in the program either at will or on certain conditions.

JUMP

The first command we will examine allows us to go to a point in the program that we select. This is the JUMP command:

```
JP          NN
```

where NN is the memory location that we want. If you have had any experience in BASIC, this is the same as the GOTO instruction.

There are two ways to JUMP to a location in assembly language but only one in machine language. Before I tell you about these, I must tell you that the only way you will get back is to JUMP back. When you use a JUMP, you can't use a RETURN to get back to the next instruction. (RETURNs will be discussed later.)

The first way to JUMP is to specify the location in hex. This is the method that you must use in machine language. It is permissible in assembly language, but there is an easier way.

This is one of the reasons that we use labels. You can actually achieve a JUMP by JUMPING to a label. When the assembler encounters a JUMP to a label, it automatically calculates the memory location of the first address of the label. Then it converts the label to the address. This is much easier on the assembly-language programmer, since it does not require that each location be calculated, in order to be plugged into the instruction. Following are some examples of the two types of JUMPS.

If the Program Counter is at location 5000H, and the instruction

```
JP      4000H
```

is encountered, then the program will automatically stop execution at location 5000H, and move to the instruction at 4000H.

Another way this could be done is if we had a label, called HERE, and that the memory location of the first instruction in the HERE routine was located at 653FH. Let's also say that the Program Counter is pointing to memory location 45A4H. If the instruction at 45A4H is

```
JP      HERE
```

the Program Counter will automatically go to location 653FH, and the instruction at 653FH will be executed.

The next JUMP instruction is called a CONDITIONAL JUMP. When the computer encounters a CONDITIONAL JUMP, it will only go to the location specified by the JUMP if the condition is met.

The conditions that are recognized are shown in Table 15-1.

In the last chapter we said that the Z flag in the F register would complement the condition of the bit. If the condition of the bit was 1, then the Z flag would be SET. Then we could execute the command JP Z,HERE. In this case HERE would be the LABEL of a subroutine. For the heck of it, let's see how those two instructions would work together.

```
BIT     3H          ;test bit 3 of the H register
JP      Z,HERE      ;JUMP to HERE if BIT 3.H is 1
```

Table 15-1. Conditional JUMPs.

CONDITION	RELEVANT FLAG
NZ (Non Zero)	Z
Z (Zero)	Z
NC (No Carry)	C
C (Carry)	C
PO (Parity Odd)	P/V
PE (Parity Even)	P/V
P (Sign Positive)	S
M (Sign Negative)	S

JUMP RELEVANT

Here is a more difficult command. This instruction tells the computer to JUMP RELEVANT, or JR. It is followed by the displacement that the computer is to JUMP. This displacement begins at the location following the instruction, and execution resumes at the next location after the displacement. This causes the program to skip over the number of locations specified by the displacement.

For example, the Program Counter is at location 5000H, and the instruction in location 5000H is JR 5. (This would take up two locations: 5000H would contain the JR instruction, and 5001H would contain the displacement of 5.) The Program Counter would start at location 5002H and skip 5002H, 5003H, 5004H, 5005H, and 5006H. The program would then resume at location 5007H.

There are two cautions here. I don't recommend that a beginner use the JR instruction because if you JUMP into the middle of an instruction, you will wipe out the entire program. This is because both numbers and instructions are coded in hex. There is a coded instruction that will correspond to any hex number stored in any location. Therefore, if you JUMPed into a number—let's say it was displacement of another JR—the computer would treat the displacement like an op-code and do whatever that op-code said to do. This would change the entire program.

The second caution I have about the use of this instruction is that you can only JUMP Relevant backwards 126 locations and forwards 129 locations.

If you goof up in machine language, you will cause a fatal program error (one that will cause the program not to run, or bomb). If you made the same mistake with the assembler, and told the Program Counter to JR to a label that was out of range, the assembler would alert you to that fact. In that case you could easily change the JR to JP.

In the back of this book there is a listing of the JUMP RELEVANT displacements that are legal. This will not only help you to program displacements in machine language, but it will also help you to trace the program if you ever need to use a T-BUG on it.

There are 4 other possible conditional JUMP RELEVANT commands. They are:

```
JR      C,D
JR      NC,D
JR      Z,D
JR      NZ,D
```

In these instructions the D stands for the displacement of the JUMP RELEVANT. With the exception that it is a JUMP RELEVANT, the conditions that must be met for the JUMP to be executed are the same as in the JP command.

There is one more type of JUMP that we will be interested in. In this JUMP, we will move to the address contained in a register pair. There are only three register pairs we can use to store the location for this JUMP. They are HL, IX, and IY. These instructions look like this:

```
JP      (HL)
JP      (IX)
JP      (IY)
```

When the computer encounters these instructions, the JUMP is made to the location stored in these register pairs.

The last instruction is the DISPLACEMENT Jump on Non Zero or DJNZ. As the name implies, it is a DISPLACEMENT jump if a non zero condition is present.

To test whether there is a zero or not, the computer checks the contents of the B register. If the contents of the B register are not zero, then the contents of the B register is decremented, and the displacement JUMP is executed. However if the contents of the B register is zero, then the next instruction is executed. Here's an example:

```
        LD    A,0H     ;set A register to zero
        LD    H,05H    ;store 5 in the H register
        LD    B,03H    ;set the number of loops
LOOP    ADD   A,H      ;A now has 5 more
        DJNZ  LOOP     ;if B is not zero do again
        JP    NEXT     ;go to the next routine
```

In the above routine, the A register is first set to zero. Then the H register is loaded with five. The B register is loaded with three. In the line labeled LOOP, the contents of H are added to the contents of the A register. For the first pass, the A register will contain 05H after the ADD is performed. Then the DJNZ instruction is executed. This decrements the contents of the B register, and then checks to see if it is zero. If not, the program then JUMPs back to the LOOP label. The contents of H (five) are ADDed to the contents of the A register. This ADD will take place four times before the B register is decremented to zero. At that point the program will fall through and execute the JUMP to the address specified by the NEXT label. In this example, the final value for A is 20H. This is one way of performing multiplication by repetitive addition.

QUIZ

1. Show how to jump to the label HERE if the test performed on the A register was zero. Show how if the test was not zero.
2. Show how to perform a JUMP RELEVANT in the question above.

ANSWERS

1. JP Z,HERE JP NZ,HERE
2. JR Z,HERE JR NZ,HERE

Chapter 16
Call and Return Group

This is the last of the instruction groups that we will cover in this book. There are two more groups, the INPUT and the OUTPUT groups, but these should only be attempted by experienced programmers.

CALL

The CALL is much like the JUMP. There is one exception. The CALL must have a RETURN to be a valid instruction. Like the UNCONDITIONAL JUMP, there are two ways of executing an UNCONDITIONAL CALL in assembly language. There is only one way in machine language. The UNCONDITIONAL CALL instruction looks like this:

```
CALL NN
```

where NN is the memory location of the subroutine that is to be executed. Here again, in assembly language we can CALL a LABEL instead of a memory location.

When a CALL is encountered, the contents of the Program Counter is PUSHed to the top of the stack. Then the Program Counter is loaded with the 2 byte memory location where execution is to begin. When a RETURN is encountered, the Stack Pointer is decremented by 3. (A CALL requires 3 bytes, 1 for the instruction and 2 for the location) and the contents is POPped into the Program Counter. This causes execution to resume at the next line after the CALL.

There is one other type of CALL, the CONDITIONAL CALL. The CONDITIONAL CALL can be executed if the contents of the F (flag) register meets the criteria of the condition required by the program. The instruction looks like this

```
CALL    CC,NN
```

where CC is the condition, and NN is the location to be CALLed.

If the condition is met, the CALL instruction is carried out the same way that it is in the UNCONDITIONAL CALL. If not, the program goes to the next line.

RETURN

Just as there are two types of CALLs, there are also two types of RETURNs. The first is the UNCONDITIONAL RETURN:

```
RET
```

When the computer encounters this type of RETURN, the Stack Pointer is decremented by 3 (a CALL requires 3 bytes, 1 for the instruction and 2 for the location) and the contents is POPped into the Program Counter. This causes execution to resume at the next line after the CALL.

The second one is the CONDITIONAL RETURN:

```
RET    CC
```

where CC is the condition. This RETURN is executed only if the condition is met. The conditions are the same as the conditional CALL conditions. Here again the F register is tested for the condition.

QUIZ

1. Show how to CALL the label HERE if the test performed on the A register was zero. Show how to CALL if the test was not zero.
2. Show how to perform a RETURN in the question above.

ANSWERS

1. CALL	Z,HERE	CALL	NZ,HERE
2. RET	Z	RET	NZ

Chapter 17
Pseudo-Ops

A pseudo-op is a special instruction used only in assembly language. This instruction does not directly affect the program, but it does give the assembler special instructions as to what we want to do.

The first one that we will look at is the ORG pseudo-op. ORG stands for ORIGINATE and tells the computer at what memory location we want to start the program. You must have an ORG statement for each assembly-language program that you write. In machine language this is not necessary as you would be programming with a T-BUG. You would start writing the program at the memory location that you wanted.

The pseudo-op goes in the op-code column, and all pseudo-ops are reserved words. This means that you can't use them for labels.

Here's what the ORG pseudo-op would look like if you wanted to start the program at 5000H.

```
100     ORG     5000H
```

After the computer encounters this instruction, which has to be the first one in the program, it will start locating the program at 5000H. This means that the first instruction would be located at 5000H, and that the leader on the tape or disc would tell the computer that the program starts at 5000H.

The ORG pseudo-op could also be labeled. When this is done, the programmer usually labels it START.

The second pseudo-op is the END instruction. It must be the last instruction in the program. The END statement is used by the assembler to locate the last memory location that the program uses for instructions. The leader of the tape or disc has the starting address, the ending address, and the starting address written on it. These addresses are followed by the name of the program.

Using the example above for the starting address, let's see what the end statement looks like.

END 5000H

or

END START

When you write a program using the T-BUG, and you're ready to save or PUNCH it onto the tape, you will use the P or PUNCH command. This is a command for the T-BUG and not for the machine language. The command that you would enter from the keyboard would look like this:

P Starting Address Ending Address Starting Address Program Name

If the starting address is 5000H, and the address of the last instruction or memory location plus one is 5C00H, and the program name is SPORTS, the P command would be carried out in this manner.

P 5000 5C00 5000 SPORTS

When you hit the enter key, the computer will write to the leader of the tape the Starting Address, the Ending Address, the Starting Address, and the file name SPORTS. It will then copy all of the contents of the locations from 5000H to 5C00H onto the tape.

Using the assembler is a different story. With the assembler, all you would have to do is type the A or ASSEMBLE instruction followed by the file name. The PUNCH operation is carried out automatically by the assembler.

When the PUNCHed program is loaded back into the computer under the SYSTEM command, the computer reads the Starting Address, the Ending Address, the Starting Address, and then it reads the file name.

Here is what it does with this information: It first checks to see if the file name on the tape matches the one that you instructed it to load. If it does, it then begins loading the information on the tape into the starting address specified on the tape. When it's done it checks to see if the ending address that it loaded the last information into, matches the one specified by the tape. If it does, it then sets the starting point for execution at the starting address specified by the tape.

The third pseudo-op is the EQUATE or EQU instruction. It can be used only once in the program for a given label. It's purpose is to set a label to a given value. For example:

```
LABEL     PSEUDO-OP     VALUE
VIDEO     EQU           3C00H
```

3C00H is the starting address of the video memory, or the first video location on the screen. Since the above instruction set the label VIDEO to 3C00H, all we have to do from now on is to use the word VIDEO in place of 3C00H (each time we want to do something with 3C00H.)

We could have just as easily used the label V instead of VIDEO. (Maybe I shouldn't tell you this for fear that you may begin to start using a lot of short cuts and confuse yourself.)

The fourth pseudo-op is the DEFL instruction. DEFL stands for DEFINE LABEL; and it sets the value of a label. It can be repeated in the program many times using different labels. The instruction looks like this:

```
LAB     DEFL     'D'
```

From now on when the computer encounters the LAB label, it will use the value for the letter D and do what is required with that letter: print it on the screen, store it somewhere, or put it on paper via the printer.

Note that in this case the D represents a letter, and not a numerical value.

The fifth pseudo-op is the DEFB or DEFINE BYTE instruction. It can be used as many times as desired in a program. DEFB can be used to generate a keyboard character without the user knowing just what the hex value of the character is. This is done by using the following instruction.

```
ONE     DEFB     31H
```

From now on when the computer encounters the word ONE, it will treat it as the character 1 (31H is the hex value of 1).

The next pseudo-op is DEFW or DEFINE WORD. This instruction is handy for working with 16-bit groups and can set a label to a hex value. For example:

```
TEN     DEFW     10H
```

Here the label TEN is used, and the pseudo-op DEFW sets the value of the word TEN to 10H. From now on, when the computer encounters the word TEN it will treat it as 10H. This case would cause the computer, when given the instruction

```
ADD     A,TEN
```

to ADD 10H to the contents of the A register.

The next pseudo-op is the DEFS or DEFINE SPACE instruction. This instruction tells the computer to reserve some space in the program for special use. If you recall the chapter about Stack Operations you will remember about the buffers that we talked about. Here's one way of creating a buffer.

```
BUFFER     DEFS     10H
```

After this instruction, 16 memory locations will be reserved for the BUFFER. Thereafter, when we tell the program to do something with the BUFFER, it will go directly to the BUFFER area.

If we inserted the DEFS 10 instruction at 5000H and labeled it BUFFER, the area from 5000H to 5010H would be protected for the BUFFER.

I'd like to note here that the label BUFFER is just that, a label. We could have just as easily called it STORE, or CAT, or DOG, or NUTS.

The last pseudo-op is the DEFM or DEFINE MESSAGE instruction. It is used with a label and can be repeated as often as you like, as long as the labels have different identities.

Its purpose is to set a message to a label so that you can

load the label instead of the entire message, one letter at a time. For example, if you wanted to print the name John Doe every time the label NAME was encountered in the program as part of the operand, you would do this:

NAME DEFM 'John Doe'

Note that the message has to be enclosed in apostrophes.

You should also know that the DEFM instruction loads the hex code for the first letter in the message into the address where it starts. It then moves to the next address and loads the next letter in the message. This process is repeated until the last letter in the message has been loaded. For example, if the DEFM starts at 6000H and the message is 10 characters long, then the first character will be stored in 6000H, the second in 6001H, etc. until all 10 characters have been stored.

When the program says to load a register pair with the message, that register pair is automatically pointed to the address where the start of the message is.

I have found great use for the DEFM in creating mailing lists and menu listings for programs. A few samples of how I go about this are listed in Table 17-1.

Now when I want to print out a menu, or an instruction that lets me make an entry from the keyboard, all I have to do is load a register pair with the label. I'll give you a subroutine for this in the next section of this book.

There is one other important thing that should be pointed out here. We can EQUATE the LENGTH of the message, and use this to load another register pair with the

Table 17-1. Using the DEFM Instruction.

NAME	DEFM	'NAME'
ADR	DEFM	'ADDRESS'
CTY	DEFM	'CITY'
STA	DEFM	'STATE'
ZIP	DEFM	'ZIP CODE'
MEN	DEFM	'MENU'
F1	DEFM	'FIND ALL PERSONS WITH THE
SAME LAST NAME'		
F2	DEFM	'FIND ALL ZIP CODES IN AN
AREA'		
LIST	DEFM	'LIST ALL NAMES IN FILE'

length of the message. We know that we can't use the EQUATE more than once on the same label. The labels in the DEFM pseudo-ops have the same rule. Let's take the example of the ZIP label. The message was 'ZIP CODE'. The message length, including the space is 8. We could use the DEFB 8, or we could load the byte counter with 8. But there is an easier way.

Why not EQUATE the ZIP length? Here is how we would do it.

```
ZIPL    EQU    $-ZIP
```

When the computer receives the instruction to load the Byte Counter with the length of the ZIP message,

```
LD    BC,ZIPL
```

it will find the equated length of the ZIP message, and load that value into the BC register pair.

To clarify this EQUATE instruction, the $ means the string or message (this could be letters, numbers, or both). The – means the length. And of course, the ZIP is the label of which we are EQUATING the length. This is a good way to remember how to write the instruction. Actually the – doesn't mean length. It's a required punctuation mark. But, if you remember it as the length, you'll have an easier time.

QUIZ

1. The __________ pseudo-op tells the computer where to start.
2. The __________ pseudo-op tells the computer where to end the program.
3. The __________ pseudo-op tells the computer to set a label to a value.
4. The __________ pseudo-op tells the computer what value to give a message length.
5. The __________ pseudo-op tells the computer to give a label a numeric value.
6. The __________ pseudo-op tells the computer to give a label a hex value.
7. The __________ pseudo-op tells the computer to reserve space.
8. The __________ pseudo-op tells the computer to set a label to a message.

ANSWERS

1. ORG
2. END
3. EQU
4. DEFL
5. DEFB
6. DEFW
7. DEFS
8. DEFM

Chapter 18
Sample Programs

In this chapter we will do some sample programs. It is important to note that the comment lines are left out in these examples. This is due to the space required to write the programs. However, you will note that the pages following these programs will contain the comments in detail and that the comments will be listed line by line.

Another important thing to note is that these are just examples. They are not intended for specific use. If you had ten different people write the same program, you would probably get ten different programs that all did the same thing. Since this is the case, these are meant only as examples of one way to do these programs.

I strongly suggest that you take these programs and experiment with them and use different methods of performing the program functions.

SUBROUTINE TO CLEAR THE SCREEN

This subroutine can be used to clear the video screen. It is executed via a call to CLS. The portion of the program that clears the screen is located at 7000H, but could be located anywhere in the program. The program is given in Fig. 18-1.

Line 100 sets the ORiGin address for the program at 5000H.

```
5000                00100               ORG     5000H
5000        CD0070  00110   START       CALL    CLS
                    00130   ;THE REST OF THE PROGRAM GOES HERE
7000                00500               ORG     7000H
7000        21003C  00510   CLS         LD      HL,3C00H
7003        11013C  00520               LD      DE,3C01H
7006        010004  00530               LD      BC,400H
7009        3620    00540               LD      (HL),20H
700B        EDB0    00550               LDIR
700D        C9      00560               RET
5000                00570               END     START
00000       TOTAL ERRORS
CLS         7000
START       5000
```

Fig. 18-1. Screen Clearing Subroutine.

Line 110 CALLs the subroutine labeled CLS.

Line 120 is the start of the rest of the program. The memory location starting at this line would be 5003H.

Line 500 starts the CLS subroutine. The ORG on this line is not necessary in actual use. I put it in this example to move the addresses of the commands to the 7000H location. In actual use you would not use the ORG statement in this line. Instead you would skip to line 510.

Line 510 begins with the CLS label. This is followed by the command to load the HL register pair with 3C00H. This is the start of the video memory.

Line 520 tells the computer to load the DE register pair with 3C01H.

Line 530 tells the computer to load the BC (byte counter) register pair with 400H. 400H is the number of bytes to be filled. The length of the video screen is 400H.

Line 540 instructs the computer to load the contents of the HL register pair with 20H, the hex code for a space.

Line 550 is the LDIR or Load Decrement Increment Repeat command. As we learned when we studied this command, when the LDIR is encountered of the HL register pair are loaded into the location pointed to by the DE register pair. Then the DE register pair is incremented and the contents of the BC register pair are decremented. If decrementing the BC register pair causes it to go to zero then the next instruction is performed. If not, the command is performed again.

Line 560 tells the computer to return to the main program and resume operation at the next program line. In this case there isn't one. You may want to put a JUMP command in at line 130 to instruct the program to go back to the START label, (5000H), or to JUMP to 5003H. Jumping to 5003H would cause a 'lock up condition' to occur. The program would keep jumping from the end of the instruction to 5003H until you press the reset button, or turn the computer off.

Line 570 contains the required END statement. Note that the operand in this line is START. This operand is not required. It does help the assembler to print the assembled version on the tape.

A QUICKER WAY TO CLEAR THE SCREEN

Figure 18-2 is a quicker way to clear the screen. This program uses a ROM routine that is the same as pressing the CLEAR key, or entering CLS in BASIC.

Line 100 sets the starting address of the program at 5000H.

Line 110 calls the subroutine labeled CLS.

Line 120 is the point at which the rest of the program is inserted. The starting address for the rest of the program would be 5003H.

Line 500 sets the ORG for the CLS subroutine. Here again, as in the first example, this line is not needed in actual use.

Line 510 is the start of the CLS subroutine. Here we find the CLS label and the CALL command followed by the address of the ROM based routine to clear the screen. The address used by the ROM to do this is 01C9H. In this ROM routine, there is an automatic return.

```
5000            00100           ORG     5000H
5000    CD0070  00110   START   CALL    CLS
5003            00120;THE REST OF THE PROGRAM GOES HERE
7000            00500           ORG     7000H
7000    CDC901  00510   CLS     CALL    01C9H
7003    C9      00520           RET
5000            00530           END     START
00000   TOTAL ERRORS
CLS     7000
START   5000
```

Fig. 18-2. A Faster Screen Clear.

Line 520 instructs the computer to return to the main program.

Line 530 is the required END instruction.

QUICK PRINTER II: MACHINE-LANGUAGE DRIVER CORRECTION

In the Quick Printer II manual there is a subroutine that can be used to send data from the computer to the printer. This program is in error and a corrected version of the program is shown in Fig. 18-3.

But first, there is a new term that you should become familiar with: *driver*. A driver is a subroutine that transfers data from the CPU to an external device such as a printer, video display, tape recorder, disc drive etc.

Entry to this subroutine is via a CALL to PTRDVR. The C register should contain the byte to be sent before the CALL is executed.

Line 100 sets the starting address for the subroutine.

Line 110 loads the A register with the printer status. The printer status is found by testing the contents of memory location 37E8H. If the printer is not busy, the contents of this address will be 0.

Line 120 masks out the upper half of the contents of 37E8H, to give a true value to the contents of that location.

Line 130 compares the contents of the A register to the hex code for 0.

Line 140 causes the computer to Jump Relevant to the start of the driver if the contents of the A register are NOT ZERO. This is the line where the Quick Printer manual is in error. The instruction in the manual will cause the program to

```
5000             00100            ORG    5000H
5000    3AE837   00110   PTRDVR   LD     A,(37E8H)
5003    E6F0     00120            AND    0F0H
5005    FE30     00130            CP     30H
5007    20F7     00140            JR     NZ,PTRDVR
5009    79       00150            LD     A,C
500A    32E837   00160            LD     (37E8H),A
500D    C9       00210            RET
5000             00220            END    PTRDVR
00000   TOTAL ERRORS
PTRDVR  5000
```

Fig. 18-3. Print Driver Correction.

```
500D     0605     00170              LD      B,5
500F     05       00180     LOOP     DEC     B
5010     78       00190              LD      A,B
5011     20FC     00200              JR      NZ,LOOP
5013     C9       00210              RET
```

Fig. 18-4. Time Delay.

Jump Relevant to the start of the routine regardless of the status. There is no condition set for the jump instruction.

Line 150 loads the contents of the C register into the A register.

Line 160 loads the contents of location 37E8H with the contents of the A register. This causes the character to be printed.

Line 210 tells the computer to return to the main program.

Line 220 is the required END statement.

Notice that lines 170 through 200 are missing in this program. The reason for this is that this driver is designed to send only one byte of data to the printer. To send more than one byte to the printer, a time delay is needed.

After the data has been sent to the printer, you will need to send a carriage return. The hex code for a carriage return is 0DH. Therefore, you will have to load the C register with 0DH, and then CALL PTRDVR again to force the printer to stop receiving data and print what it already has in its stack. If the stack gets filled (it has a 32-character capacity) before the 0DH is sent, the printer will print what is in the stack, then resume loading its stack again. Figure 18-4 is a time delay that can be used to load more than one byte at a time.

Line 170 instructs the computer to load the B register with 5. This is the register that we will use to count the delay. As you can see, the address of this instruction, 500DH, is the address where the RET is located for the previous driver. This is because the delay must come before the return. Therefore, we must replace the return instruction with the first instruction in the delay.

Line 180 is the line where the delay loop actually takes place. Here the B register is decremented preparing its value for the next step.

Line 190 loads the A register with the contents of the B register, preparing it for testing. As the byte that was to be sent to the printer is no longer needed, we can load A with B and not have to worry about what will happen to the data being sent to the printer.

Line 200 tells the computer to Jump Relevant to the LOOP if the contents of the A register are not zero. If this is done, the contents of the B register will be decremented again, and the loop will be repeated. However, if the contents of the A register is zero, then the next instruction will be carried out.

Line 210 is still the return statement and acts as it did in the original driver. The only difference is the location of the instruction.

The assembled version of this routine will also include the address of the LOOP label.

ROUTINE TO FILL THE SCREEN WITH ANY CHARACTER FROM THE KEYBOARD

This routine, shown in Fig. 18-5, will allow you to enter any character from the keyboard and will fill the screen with that character.

Line 100 sets the starting point at 5000H.

Line 110 calls the ROM-based routine to clear the screen.

Line 120 calls the ROM-based routine. This routine scans the keyboard for an entry and then returns with the value of the key that was pressed, stored in the A register. If no key was pressed, then the A register will contain 00H.

Line 130 checks the value stored in the A register to see if it is zero. If it is, the Z flag in the F register is set.

Line 140 instructs the computer to jump back to the LOOP label if the Z flag is set.

Line 150 loads the HL register pair with the starting address of the video memory (3C00H).

Line 160 loads the DE register pair with the address of the second video memory location, 3C01H.

Line 170 loads the Byte Counter register pair, BC, with the number of locations to be filled with the character.

```
5000                 00100           ORG    5000H
5000    CDC901       00110   START   CALL   01C9H
5003    CD4900       00120   LOOP    CALL   049H
5006    FE00         00130           CP     00H
5008    CA0350       00140           JP     Z,LOOP
500B    21003C       00150           LD     HL,3C00H
500E    11013C       00160           LD     DE,3C01H
5011    010004       00170           LD     BC,400H
5014    77           00180           LD     (HL),A
5015    EDB0         00190           LDIR
5017    C30350       00200           JP     LOOP
5000                 00210           END    START
```

Fig. 18-5. Screen Fill Routine.

Line 180 loads the value in the A register into the address pointed to by the HL register pair.

Line 190 is the LDIR instruction. This instruction causes the contents of the memory location specified by the HL register pair to be loaded into the location specified by the DE register pair, and the contents of the BC register pair to be decremented. If decrementing the contents of the BC register pair causes it to be zero, then the program will continue to the next line. If not, the instruction will be repeated.

Line 200 causes the program counter to jump back to the LOOP label, location 5003H. This action allows you to enter another character and repeat the process. Until a key is pressed, the value returned in the A register from the call to 049H will be 0 and this will cause the program to return to 5003H.

Line 210 is the mandatory END statement. Here again we use the operand START for safety reasons.

ROUTINE TO ENTER A SPECIFIED NUMBER OF CHARACTERS FROM THE KEYBOARD

This routine (Fig. 18-6) will enable you to load a specified number of characters from the keyboard. It will continue to do so until one of these two conditions are met.

1. The break key is pressed.
2. The enter key is pressed.

We will store the characters on the screen to prove our point. Two interesting things are demonstrated here. The first is that when the last character is entered, and another is

```
5000                    00100   ORG     5000H
5000    21003C          00110   AUTO    LD      HL,3C00H
5003    060A            00120           LD      B,10
5005    CD4000          00130           CALL    40H
5008    CDC901          00140           CALL    01C9H
500B    C30050          00150           JP      AUTO
5000                    00160           END
00000   TOTAL ERRORS
AUTO    5000
```

Fig. 18-6. Keyboard Character Entry.

pressed, the last character will be replaced by the extra entry. The second thing is that the backspace key is recognized.

Line 100 sets the starting point for the program.

Line 110 contains the label AUTO and also tells the computer to load the HL register pair with the starting address of the video memory.

Line 120 loads the B register with the number of spaces to fill. You may use up to 255 (FFH). The B register is used as the Byte Counter.

Line 130 performs the call to the ROM-based scan and load routine.

Line 140 performs the call to 01C9H to clear the screen when the BREAK or ENTER key is pressed.

Line 150 causes the program to jump back to the start for the next 10 characters.

Line 160 is the mandatory END statement.

ROUTINE TO TRANSFER THE CONTENTS OF ONE MEMORY LOCATION TO ANOTHER

This routine, given in Fig. 18-7, can be used to move the contents of one location to another. To demonstrate this, we will move the contents of a buffer to the screen.

Line 100 sets the starting address for the program.

Line 110 calls the ROM-based function to clear the screen. This line is also labeled START.

Line 120 instructs the computer to load the DE register pair with the starting address of the screen.

Line 130 instructs the computer to load the HL register pair with the address of the buffer. In this program the label BUFFER is located at 5011H, so the HL register is loaded with 5011H.

Line 140 loads the Byte Counter, the BC register pair, with the number of locations having contents to be transferred. In this case we want to transfer the contents of 16 locations. It should be noted that the contents of these locations, which is the BUFFER, will not be altered. You can prove this by loading and running the program with a T-BUG. In doing this you can set a break point using the B command in the T-BUG at 500EH. When the program encounters the break point, it will return a # sign. At the same time you should type in an M followed by the address of the buffer, 5011H. You will see that the contents of the 16 locations in the buffer have not changed.

Line 150 is the LDIR command. This command is the heart of the routine. It performs the transfer.

Line 160 is the loop line.

When the transfer is complete, the jump to LOOP keeps the program from going to an unwanted instruction somewhere in the stack. Here is a good example of what we said earlier about an invalid instruction being executed. If you look up the numeric instruction listing for the codes 41H through

```
5000              00100                ORG     5000H
5000   CDC901     00110   START        CALL    01C9H
5003   11003C     00120                LD      DE,3C00H
5006   211150     00130                LD      HL,BUFFER
5009   012400     00140                LD      BC,16
500C   EDB0       00150                LDIR
500E   C30E50     00160   LOOP         JP      LOOP
5011   41         00170   BUFFER       DEFM    'ABCDEFGHIJKLMNOP'
5012   42
5013   43
5014   44
5015   45
5016   46
5017   47
5018   48
5019   49
501A   4A
501B   4B
501C   4C
501D   4D
501E   4E
501F   4F
5020   50
5000              00180                END     START
00000  TOTAL ERRORS
BUFFER 5011
LOOP   500E
START  5000
```

Fig. 18-7. Memory Location Contents Transfer.

50H, you will discover that these are load instructions for the B, C, and D registers. If the loop were there, and the program counter were not redirected to location 5003H, these loads would be performed and the computer would go into hyperspace. Eventually, it would reach a CALL or JUMP to 00H. This would cause it to return to the power-up state and print the message MEMORY SIZE.

Line 170 not only provides the BUFFER label, but also provides the data for the buffer. In this case we used the DEFM pseudo-op, but we could have stored the information in the buffer from the keyboard or any type of input device.

Line 180 is the required END statement.

PROGRAM TO PRINT A MAILING LIST

This routine, shown in Fig. 18-8, prints out a mailing list. In this example we will store the data in a data buffer. In actual usage you would probably use an I/O (Input/Output) device to store the information. This program also uses delimiters to separate the various pieces of data. A delimiter is a character that you will not be using in the data. In this case, we will use a) sign to show the end of the data listing for each person, and a (sign to separate the various pieces of data for any given person.

For the purpose of shortening this program description, we will skip over the parts of this program that we have outlined in the previous program and concentrate on the new parts of the program.

Line 100 sets the starting point for the program. Line 110 CALLs the ROM function to clear the screen.

Lines 120 through 350 print out the message 'NAME' 'ADDRESS' 'STREET' 'CITY' 'STATE' and 'ZIP CODE'. They also set the video locations in the DE register pair and the length of the messages in the BC register pair. After this is done, they perform the LDIR command. The messages are numbered M1 through M6. The video settings for these lines are numbered V1 through V6. The message lengths for these lines are equated at the length of the messages. These lengths are labeled M1L through M6L. This pro-

```
5000            00100           ORG     5000H
5000   CDC901   00110   START   CALL    01C9H
5003   11003C   00120           LD      DE,V1
5006   21AA50   00130           LD      HL,M1
5009   010400   00140           LD      BC,M1L
500C   EDB0     00150           LDIR
500E   11403C   00160           LD      DE,V2
5011   21AE50   00170           LD      HL,M2
5014   010600   00180           LD      BC,M2L
5017   EDB0     00190           LDIR
5019   11803C   00200           LD      DE,V3
501C   21B550   00210           LD      HL,M3
501F   010600   00220           LD      BC,M3L
5022   EDB0     00230           LDIR
5024   11C03C   00240           LD      DE,V4
5027   21BB50   00250           LD      HL,M4
502A   010400   00260           LD      BC,M4L
502D   EDB0     00270           LDIR
502F   11003D   00280           LD      DE,V5
5032   21BF50   00290           LD      HL,M5
5035   010500   00300           LD      BC,M5L
5038   EDB0     00310           LDIR
503A   11403D   00320           LD      DE,V6
503D   21C450   00340           LD      HL,M6
5040   010800   00350           LD      BC,M6L
5043   EDB0     00360           LDIR
5045   21CC50   00370           LD      HL,DATA
5048   110A3C   00380           LD      DE,V7
504B   7E       00390   LP1     LD      A,(HL)
504C   FE28     00400           CP      28H
504E   CA5750   00410           JP      Z,LP2
5051   12       00420           LD      (DE),A
5052   13       00430           INC     DE
5053   23       00440           INC     HL
5054   C34B50   00450           JP      LP1
5057   23       00460   LP2     INC     HL
5058   114A3C   00470           LD      DE,V8
505B   7E       00480   LP2A    LD      A,(HL)
505C   FE28     00490           CP      28H
505E   CA6750   00500           JP      Z,LP3
5061   12       00510           LD      (DE),A
5062   13       00520           INC     DE
5063   23       00530           INC     HL
5064   C35B50   00540           JP      LP2A
5067   118A3C   00550   LP3     LD      DE,V9
506A   23       00560           INC     HL
506B   7E       00570   LP3A    LD      A,(HL)
506C   FE28     00580           CP      28H
506E   CA7750   00590           JP      Z,LP4
5071   12       00600           LD      (DE),A
5072   13       00610           INC     DE
```

Fig. 18-8. Mailing List.

```
5073  23              INC   HL
5074  C36B50          JP    LP3A
5077  11CA3C    LP4   LD    DE,V10
507A  23              INC   HL
507B  7E        LP4A  LD    A,(HL)
507C  FE28            CP    28H
507E  CA8A50          JP    Z,LP5
5081  12              LD    (DE),A
5082  13              INC   DE
5083  23              INC   HL
5084  C37B50          JP    LP4A
5087  23        LP5   INC   HL
5088  110A3D          LD    DE,V11
508B  7E        LP5A  LD    A,(HL)
508C  FE28            CP    28H
508E  CA5097          JP    Z,LP6
5091  12              LD    (DE),A
5092  13              INC   DE
5093  23              INC   HL
5094  C38B50          JP    LP5A
5097  23        LP6   INC   HL
5098  114A3D          LD    DE,V12
509B  7E        LP6A  LD    A,(HL)
509C  FE29            CP    29H
509E  CAA750          JP    Z,STOP
50A1  12              LD    (DE),A
50A2  13              INC   DE
50A3  23              INC   HL
50A4  C39B50          JP    LP6A
50A7  C3A750    STOP  JP    STOP
3C00            V1    EQU   3C00H
3C40            V2    EQU   V1+64
3C80            V3    EQU   V2+64
3CC0            V4    EQU   V3+64
3D00            V5    EQU   V4+64
3D40            V6    EQU   V5+64
3C0A            V7    EQU   V1+10
3C4A            V8    EQU   V2+10
3C8A            V9    EQU   V3+10
3CCA            V10   EQU   V4+10
3D0A            V11   EQU   V5+10
3D4A            V12   EQU   V6+10
50AA  4E        M1    DEFM  'NAME'
50AB  41
50AC  4D
50AD  45
50AE  41        M2    DEFM  'ADDRESS'
50AF  44
50B0  44
50B1  52
50B2  45
```

Fig. 18-8. Continued from page 133.

```
50B3    53
50B4    53
50B5    53      01060   M3      DEFM   'STREET'
50B6    54
50B7    52
50B8    45
50B9    45
50BA    54
50BB    43      01070   M4      DEFM   'CITY'
50BC    49
50BD    54
50BE    59
50BF    53      01080   M5      DEFM   'STATE'
50C0    54
50C1    41
50C2    54
50C3    45
50C4    5A      01090   M6      DEFM   'ZIP CODE'
50C5    49
50C6    50
50C7    20
50C8    43
50C9    4F
50CA    44
50CB    45
0004            01100   M1L     EQU    $-M1
0007            01110   M2L     EQU    $-M2
0006            01120   M3L     EQU    $-M3
0004            01130   M4L     EQU    $-M4
0005            01140   M5L     EQU    $-M5
0008            01150   M6L     EQU    $-M6
50CC    59      01160   DATA    DEFM   'YOUR NAME
(123(S. WEST AVE(ANYTOWN(CA(12345)'
50CD    4F
50CE    55
50CF    52
50D0    20
50D1    4E
50D2    41
50D3    4D
50D4    45
50D5    28
50D6    31
50D7    32
50D8    33
50D9    28
50DA    53
50DB    2E
50DC    2E
50DD    57
50DE    45
```

```
50DF        53
50E0        54
50E1        20
50E2        41
50E3        56
50E4        45
50E5        28
50E6        41
50E7        4E
50E8        59
50E9        54
50EA        4F
50EB        57
50EC        4E
50ED        28
50EE        43
503F        41
50F0        28
50F1        31
50F2        32
50F3        33
50F4        34
50F5        35
50F6        29
5000                  01170    END      START
00000       TOTAL ERRORS
LP6A        509B
V12         3D4A
LP6         5097
LP5A        508B
V11         3D0A
STOP        50A7
LP5         50A8
LP4A        50B7
V10         3CCA
LP4         5077
LP3A        506B
V9          3CBA
LP3         5067
LP2A        505B
V8          3C4A
LP2         5057
LP1         504B
V7          3C0A
DATA        50CF
M6L         0008
M6          50C7
V6          3D40
M5L         0005
M5          50C2
V5          3D00
M4L         0004
```

Fig. 18-8. Continued from page 135.

```
M4      50BE
V4      3CC0
M3L     0006
M3      50BB
V3      3CB0
M2L     0007
M2      50B1
V2      3C40
M1L     0004
M1      50AD
V1      3C00
START   5000
```

Fig. 18-8. (Continued from page 136.)

gram uses a special technique to set the video locations that will be discussed later in the description of this program.

Line 360 is the start of the portion of the program that prints out the data to the screen. Here the HL register pair is loaded with the label DATA. This label is located at the address in which the first byte of the data is stored. As we said earlier, the data for this program is stored in a DEFM statement. However, if we wanted to, we could load the data from an external source by storing it into a BUFFER. If you decide to do this, all that would be required would be a subroutine to load the data into the address specified by the DATA label. After this is done, you could proceed with the program starting at line 360. *Caution:* Some alteration would be required since this program is only designed to receive one data line. I would suggest using a third delimiter to signify the end of the available data. Then add a routine to test for that delimiter.

Line 370 loads the DE register pair with the video address where the first piece of data is to be printed.

Line 380 begins the loop to check for the first delimiter. Here the contents of the HL register pair are loaded into the A register.

Line 390 checks the contents of the A register for 28H. 28H is the (sign. It acts as our end-of-line delimiter.

Line 400 instructs the computer to JUMP to the start of the search/print routine for the next line (if the delimiter is found).

Line 410 loads the character in the A register, (the one that we got from the HL register pair) into the address specified by the DE register pair.

Line 420 causes the DE register pair to be incremented.

Line 430 causes the HL register pair to be incremented.

Line 440 causes the program to JUMP back to the loop, in this case LP1, and test for the next character. This process is repeated from line 450 through line 900. The only difference is that in line 880 a test is made for the) sign which is 29H. Line 890 causes the program to JUMP to line 910, or the stop label, if a true comparison occurs.

Line 910 causes the computer to lock up in a protective loop at the end of the program.

Line 920 sets the value given to V1 at 3C00H. This value is also in the DE register pair. There are many ways of setting the video address where information is to be printed. I chose this one to show you a little variety. Also, this is a convenient way to indicate lines and tabs without having to do computations by hand, or adding to the hex address 3 or 4 times.

Line 930 starts our short cut to setting the starting point for the data in M2 to M6. We have already EQUated the value of V1 at 3C00H. We can now set V2 to the start of the next line by EQUating V2 as V1+64 (there are 63 characters per line). The same will hold true for V3 if we EQUate V3 as V2+64. This is permissible as long as we have previously set the value of the label that we are adding to.

Line 980 starts the tab function. You could use the ROM-based tab function but remember that function tabs in increments of 8. Here we wanted to tab in increments of 10. The values of V1 through V6 have already been set, and we just want to tab over 10 spaces each time. All we have to do is set a different label for that particular line and tab. EQUate that label as the video line label + 10. As we can see, V7, the video location where we wanted to print the person's name, was EQUated as V1, the video line number, + 10, the number of spaces to tab over. It is not necessary to use V1 to label the first video line. I did it this way to keep track more easily. I said to myself, the V will stand for VIDEO and the line number. As there were only 6 categories that I wanted to print out, I started with 7 for the information lines. Now that I think about it, it would have been just as easy, if not easier to use I1 instead of V7. The I would stand for Information. If I wanted to get real fancy, I could have used the label IL1 for Information line 1.

Line 1040 is where the addresses of the category headings are started. Here we set the label M1 using the DEFM pseudo-op to 'NAME'. The same holds true for line 1050 through line 1090.

Lines 1100 through 1150 use the EQUate pseudo-op to set the length of the labels M1 to M6. Here I used the label and added the letter L to tell me that was the length of the label. This made it easier when I was writing the program, since, when I was working with V1 and M1, I would not use the wrong number to load the BC register pair with. I would instead load the BC register pair with M1L, or the length of message 1.

Line 1160 sets the address for the start of our data buffer. This buffer is labeled DATA. For the purposes of demonstration, I used the DEFM pseudo-op to enter the data in the buffer.

Line 1700 is the required END statement.

HARD BUG

This program (Fig. 18-9) will provide you with a hard copy (a written copy) of the contents of a specified group of memory locations. Along with their contents, the location is also printed out. After loading the program under the SYSTEM command, enter a / followed by pressing the ENTER key.

The program will respond by asking you at what address you want to start printing. Enter the hex value of the address. The program will then ask you at what address you want to stop. Enter the ending address + 1 in hex and then sit back. The printer and CPU will do the rest.

When you run this program for the first time try using 3C00 for the starting address and 3C0B for the ending address. After the printer is done, compare the printed hex values in these locations to the hex codes for the first 10 characters on the screen.

Line 100 sets the starting address of the program.

Line 110 CALLS the ROM routine to clear the screen.

```
5000                        ORG     5000H
5000    CDC901                      CALL    01C9H
5003    11003C                      LD      DE,3C00H
5006    216152                      LD      HL,MESS1
5009    011400                      LD      BC,20
500C    EDB0                        LDIR
500E    D5              PRINT1      PUSH    DE
500F    CDAF51                      CALL    SCAN
5012    D1                          POP     DE
5013    12                          LD      (DE),A
5014    13                          INC     DE
5015    78              P1A         LD      A,B
5016    FE00                        CP      0
5018    281F                        JR      Z,P1B
501A    210000                      LD      HL,0000H
501D    225B52                      LD      (STABUF),HL
5020    225D52                      LD      (ENDBUF),HL
5023    225F52                      LD      (TOTBUF),HL
5026    2A5B52                      LD      HL,(STABUF)
5029    D5                          PUSH    DE
502A    ED5B8952                    LD      DE,(TABLE)
502E    19              P1L1        ADD     HL,DE
502F    05                          DEC     B
5030    78                          LD      A,B
5031    FE00                        CP      0
5033    20F9                        JR      NZ,P1L1
5035    22B552                      LD      (STABUF),HL
5038    D1                          POP     DE
5039    D5              P1B         PUSH    DE
503A    CDAF51                      CALL    SCAN
503D    D1                          POP     DE
503E    12                          LD      (DE),A
503F    13                          INC     DE
5040    78                          LD      A,B
5041    FE00                        CP      0
5043    2813                        JR      Z,PC1
5045    D5                          PUSH    DE
5046    ED5B8B52                    LD      DE,(TABLE2)
504A    2AB552                      LD      HL,(STABUF)
504D    19              P1L2        ADD     HL,DE
504E    05                          DEC     B
504F    78                          LD      A,B
5050    FE00                        CP      0
5052    20F9                        JR      NZ,P1L2
5054    225B52                      LD      (STABUF),HL
5057    D1                          POP     DE
5058    D5              P1C         PUSH    DE
5059    CDAF51                      CALL    SCAN
505C    D1                          POP     DE
505D    12                          LD      (DE),A
505E    13                          INC     DE
505F    78                          LD      A,B
5060    FE00                        CP      0
5062    2813                        JR      Z,P1D
5064    D5                          PUSH    DE
5065    ED5B8D52                    LD      DE,(TABLE3)
5069    2A5B52                      LD      HL,(STABUF)
```

Fig. 18-9. Hard Copy Routine.

```
506C  19               P1L3    ADD     HL,DE
506D  05                       DEC     B
506E  78                       LD      A,B
506F  FE00                     CP      0
5071  20F9                     JR      Z,P1L3
5073  D1                       POP     DE
5074  225B52                   LD      (STABUF),HL
5077  D5               P1D     PUSH    DE
5078  CDAF51                   CALL    SCAN
507B  D1                       POP     DE
507C  12                       LD      (DE),A
507D  78                       LD      A,B
507E  FE00                     CP      0
5080  2811                     JR      Z,PRINT2
5082  ED5B8F52                 LD      DE,(TABLE4)
5086  2A5B52                   LD      HL,(STABUF)
5089  19               P1L4    ADD     HL,DE
508A  05                       DEC     B
508B  78                       LD      A,B
508C  FE00                     CP      0
508E  20F9                     JR      NZ,P1L4
5090  225B52                   LD      (STABUF),HL
5093  217552           PRINT2  LD      HL,MESS2
5096  11803C                   LD      DE,3C00H+128
5099  011400                   LD      BC,20
509C  EDB0                     LDIR
509E  D5                       PUSH    DE
509F  CDAF51                   CALL    SCAN
50A2  D1                       POP     DE
50A3  12                       LD      (DE),A
50A4  13                       INC     DE
50A5  78               P2A     LD      A,B
50A6  FE00                     CP      0
50A8  2813                     JR      Z,P2B
50AA  2A5D52                   LD      HL,(ENDBUF)
50AD  D5                       PUSH    DE
50AE  ED5B8952                 LD      DE,(TABLE1)
50B2  19               P2L1    ADD     HL,DE
50B3  05                       DEC     B
50B4  78                       LD      A,B
50B5  FE00                     CP      0
50B7  20F9                     JR      NZ,P2L1
50B9  225D52                   LD      (ENDBUF),HL
50BC  D1                       POP     DE
50BD  D5               P2B     PUSH    DE
50BE  CDAF51                   CALL    SCAN
50C1  D1                       POP     DE
50C2  12                       LD      (DE),A
50C3  13                       INC     DE
50C4  78                       LD      A,B
50C5  FE00                     CP      0
50C7  2813                     JR      Z,P2C
50C9  D5                       PUSH    DE
50CA  ED5B8B52                 LD      DE,(TABLE2)
50CE  2A5D52                   LD      HL,(ENDBUF)
50D1  19               P2L2    ADD     HL,DE
50D2  05                       DEC     B
```

```
50D3   78                   LD      A,B
50D4   FE00                 CP      0
50D6   20F9                 JR      NZ,P2L2
50D8   225D52               LD      (ENDBUF),HL
50DB   D1                   POP     DE
50DC   D5          P2C      PUSH    DE
50DD   CDAF51               CALL    SCAN
50E0   D1                   POP     DE
50E1   12                   LD      (DE),A
50E2   13                   INC     DE
50E3   78                   LD      A,B
50E4   FE00                 CP      0
50E6   2813                 JR      Z,P2D
50E8   D5                   PUSH    DE
50E9   ED5B8D52             LD      DE,(TABLE3)
50ED   2A5D52               LD      HL,(ENDBUF)
50F0   19          P2L3     ADD     HL,DE
50F1   05                   DEC     B
50F2   78                   LD      A,B
50F3   FE00                 CP      0
50F5   20F9                 JR      NZ,P2L3
50F7   225D52               LD      (ENDBUF),HL
50FA   D1                   POP     DE
50FB   D5          P2D      PUSH    DE
50FC   CDAF51               CALL    SCAN
50FF   D1                   POP     DE
5100   12                   LD      (DE),A
5101   78                   LD      A,B
5102   FE00                 CP      0
5104   2811                 JR      Z,PRINT3
5106   ED5B8F52             LD      DE,(TABLE4)
510A   2A5D52               LD      HL,(ENDBUF)
510D   19          P2L4     ADD     HL,DE
510E   05                   DEC     B
510F   78                   LD      A,B
5110   FE00                 CP      0
5112   20F9                 JR      NZ,P2L4
5114   225D52               LD      (ENDBUF),HL
5117   11003C      PRINT3   LD      DE,3C00H
511A   0618                 LD      B,24
511C   C5          P3L1     PUSH    BC
511D   1A                   LD      A,(DE)
511E   4F                   LD      C,A
511F   CD4752               CALL    POUT
5122   13                   INC     DE
5123   C1                   POP     BC
5124   05                   DEC     B
5125   78                   LD      A,B
5126   FE00                 CP      0
5128   20F2                 JR      NZ,P3L1
512A   0E0D                 LD      C,0DH
512C   CD4752               CALL    POUT
512F   CD4752               CALL    POUT
5132   11803C               LD      DE,3C00H+128
5135   0618                 LD      B,24
5137   C5          P3L2     PUSH    BC
5138   1A                   LD      A,(DE)
```

Fig. 18-9. Continued from page 141.

```
5139   4F                     LD     C,A
513A   CD4752                 CALL   POUT
513D   13                     INC    DE
513E   C1                     POP    BC
513F   05                     DEC    B
5140   78                     LD     A,B
5141   FE00                   CP     0
5143   20F2                   JR     NZ,P3L2
5145   0E0D                   LD     C,0DH
5147   CD4752                 CALL   POUT
514A   0620                   LD     B,32
514C   C5         P3L3        PUSH   BC
514D   0E2D                   LD     C,2DH
514F   CD4752                 CALL   POUT
5152   C1                     POP    BC
5153   05                     DEC    B
5154   78                     LD     A,B
5155   FE00                   CP     0
5157   20F3                   JR     NZ,P3L3
5159   0E0D                   LD     C,0DH
515B   CD4752                 CALL   POUT
515E   2A5D52     PREP3       LD     HL,(ENDBUF)
5161   ED5B5B52               LD     DE,(STABUF)
5165   ED52                   SBC    HL,DE
5167   225F52                 LD     (TOTBUF),HL
516A   ED4B5F52               LD     BC,(TOTBUF)
516E   ED5B5B52               LD     DE,(STABUF)
5172   C5         START       PUSH   BC
5173   7A                     LD     A,D
5174   CD2852                 CALL   HEXCV
5177   4C                     LD     C,H
5178   CD4752                 CALL   POUT
517B   4D                     LD     C,L
517C   CD4752                 CALL   POUT
517F   7B                     LD     A,E
5180   CD2852                 CALL   HEXCV
5183   4C                     LD     C,H
5184   CD4752                 CALL   POUT
5187   4D                     LD     C,L
5188   CD4752                 CALL   POUT
518B   0E20                   LD     C,20H
518D   CD4752                 CALL   POUT
5190   CD4752                 CALL   POUT
5193   1A                     LD     A,(DE)
5194   CD2852                 CALL   HEXCV
5197   4C                     LD     C,H
5198   CD4752                 CALL   POUT
519B   4D                     LD     C,L
519C   CD4752                 CALL   POUT
519F   0E0D                   LD     C,0DH
51A1   CD4752                 CALL   POUT
51A4   13                     INC    DE
51A5   C1                     POP    BC
51A6   0B                     DEC    BC
51A7   78                     LD     A,B
51A8   B1                     OR     C
```

```
51A9     C27251    02370           JP      NZ,START
51AC     C30050    02380           JP      5000H
51AF     3E23      02390   SCAN    LD      A,23H
51B1     12        02400           LD      (DE),A
51B2     D5        02410           PUSH    DE
51B3     CD4900    02420           CALL    049H
51B6     D1        02430           POP     DE
51B7     FE30      02440           CP      30H
51B9     2003      02450           JR      NZ,S1
51BB     0600      02460           LD      B,0
51BD     C9        02470           RET
51BE     FE31      02480   S1      CP      31H
51C0     2003      02490           JR      NZ,S2
51C2     0601      02500           LD      B,1
51C4     C9        02510           RET
51C5     FE32      02520   S2      CP      32H
51C7     2003      02530           JR      NZ,S3
51C9     0602      02540           LD      B,2
51CB     C9        02550           RET
51CC     FE33      02560   S3      CP      33H
51CE     2003      02570           JR      NZ,S4
51D0     0603      02580           LD      B,3
51D2     C9        02590           RET
51D3     FE34      02600   S4      CP      34H
51D5     2003      02610           JR      NZ,S5
51D7     0604      02620           LD      B,4
51D9     C9        02630           RET
51DA     FE35      02640   S5      CP      35H
51DC     2003      02650           JR      NZ,S6
51DE     0605      02660           LD      B,5
51E0     C9        02670           RET
51E1     FE36      02680   S6      CP      36H
51E3     2003      02690           JR      NZ,S7
51E5     0606      02700           LD      B,6
51E7     C9        02710           RET
51E8     FE37      02720   S7      CP      37H
51EA     2003      02730           JR      NZ,S8
51EC     0607      02740           LD      B,7
51EE     C9        02750           RET
51EF     FE38      02760   S8      CP      38H
51F1     2003      02770           JR      NZ,S9
51F3     0608      02780           LD      B,8
51F5     C9        02790           RET
51F6     FE39      02800   S9      CP      39H
51F8     2003      02810           JR      NZ,SA
51FA     0609      02820           LD      B,9
51FC     C9        02830           RET
51FD     FE41      02840   SA      CP      41H
51FF     2003      02850           JR      NZ,SN
5201     060A      02860           LD      B,10
5203     C9        02870           RET
5204     FE42      02880   SB      CP      42H
5206     2003      02890           JR      NZ,SC
5208     030B      02900           LD      B,11
520A     C9        02910           RET
520B     FE43      02920   SC      CP      43H
520D     2003      02930           JR      NZ.SD
```

Fig. 18-9. Continued from page 143.

```
520F   060C               LD     B,12
5211   C9                 RET
5212   FE44     SD        CP     44H
5214   2003               JR     NZ,SE
5216   060D               LD     B,13
5218   C9                 RET
5219   FE45     SE        CP     45H
521B   2003               JR     NZ,SF
521D   600E               LD     B,14
521F   C9                 RET
5220   FE46     SF        CP     46H
5222   C2AF51             JP     NZ,SCAN
5225   060F               LD     B,15
5227   C9                 RET
5228   4F       HEXCV     LD     C,A
5229   CB3F               SRL    A
522B   CB3F               SRL    A
522D   CB3F               SRL    A
522F   CB3F               SRL    A
5231   CD3D52             CALL   TEST
5234   67                 LD     H,A
5235   79                 LD     A,C
5236   E60F               AND    0FH
5238   CD3D52             CALL   TEST
523B   6F                 LD     L,A
523C   C9                 RET
523D   C630     TEST      ADD    A,30H
523F   FE3A               CP     3AH
5241   FA4652             JP     M,TEST1
5244   C607               ADD    A,7
5246   C9       TEST1     RET
5247   3AE837   POUT      LD     A,(37E8H)
524A   E6F0               AND    0F0H
524C   FE30               CP     30H
524E   20F7               JR     NZ,POUT
5250   79                 LD     A,C
5251   32E837             LD     (37E8H),A
5254   0605               LD     B,5
5256   05       POUT1     DEC    B
5257   78                 LD     A,B
5258   20FC               JR     NZ,POUT1
525A   C9                 RET
0002            STABUF    DEFS   2
0002            ENDBUF    DEFS   2
0002            TOTBUF    DEFS   2
5261   53       MESS1     DEFM   'STARTING
                                 ADDRESS
5262   54
5263   41
5264   52
5265   54
5266   49
5267   4E
5268   47
5269   20
526A   41
```

```
526B      44
526C      44
526D      52
526E      45
526F      53
5270      53
5271      20
5272      20
5273      20
5274      20
5275      45        03400     MESS2     DEFM      'ENDING
 ,                                                 ADDRESS
5276      4E
5277      44
5278      49
5279      4E
527A      47
527B      20
527C      41
527D      44
527E      44
527F      52
5280      45
5281      53
5282      53
5283      20
5284      20
5285      20
5286      20
5287      20
5288      20
5289      0010      03410     TABLE1    DEFW      1000H
528B      0001      03420     TABLE2    DEFW      0100H
528D      1000      03430     TABLE3    DEFW      0010H
528F      0100      03440     TABLE4    DEFW      0001H
0000                03450               END
00000     TOTAL ERRORS
POUT1     5256
TEST1     5246
TEST      523D
SF        5220
SE        5219
SD        5212
SC        520B
SB        5204
SA        51FD
S9        51F6
S8        51EF
S7        51E8
S6        51E1
S5        51DA
S4        51D3
S3        51CC
S2        51C5
S1        51BE
HEXCV     5228
START     5172
```

Fig. 18-9. Continued from page 145.

```
PREP3     515E
P3L3      514C
P3L2      5137
POUT      5247
P3L1      511C
P2L4      510D
PRINT3    5111
P2L3      50F0
P2D       50FB
P2L2      50D1
P2C       50DC
P2L1      50B2
P2B       50BD
P2A       50A5
MESS2     5275
P1L4      5089
TABLE4    528F
PRINT2    5093
P1L3      506C
TABLE3    528D
P1D       5077
P1L2      504D
TABLE2    528B
P1C       5058
P1L1      502E
TABLE1    5289
TOTBUF    525F
ENDBUF    525D
STABUF    525B
P1B       5039
P1A       5015
SCAN      51AF
PRINT1    500E
MESS1     5261
```

Fig. 18-9. (Continued from page 146.)

Lines 120 through 150 sets up and prints the message for the user to enter the starting address.

Line 160 is the start of the PRINT1 routine. Here DE is PUSHed because, the DE register pair is used in the ROM for the next line.

Line 170 CALLs the SCAN subroutine.

Line 180 POPs DE back again.

Line 190 loads the value in the A register (it was picked up in the scan routine) into the location specified by the DE register pair.

Line 200 increments the DE register pair to the next video location.

Line 210 is the start of the P1A loop. Here the A register is loaded with the contents of the B register. This will be where the value for the starting address is computed and stored. The B register will hold the multiplier. It obtained its value from the SCAN routine.

Line 220 compares the value in the A register for zero.

Line 230 causes a JUMP to P1B if the value in A is zero.

Line 240 loads the HL register pair with zero. This will be used in lines 250 through 270 to preset the values of the start buffer (STABUF), the end buffer (ENDBUF) and the total buffer (TOTBUF), to zero. TOTBUF will contain the number of bytes to be sent to the printer.

Line 280 loads the HL register pair with the contents of STABUF.

Line 290 saves the present value of DE.

Line 300 loads the DE register pair with the value in TABLE1.

Line 310 is the start of the addition loop. The contents of the DE register pair (containing the table) are repeatedly added to the HL register pair (containing the current total) in the STABUF. After each addition is performed, the B register is decremented and checked for zero. If it is not zero, the routine is repeated. If it is zero the next routine is executed. This picks up the next hex digit and adds its value to the buffer. The loop ends on line 360 where STABUF is loaded with the contents of the HL register pair. The loading of STABUF is completed on line 880.

Lines 890 through 1610 are a repetition of lines 120 through 880. The only difference is that these lines work with ENDBUF instead of STABUF.

Lines 1620 through 1760 send the contents of the first video line to the printer. They end by sending 2 carriage returns to the printer to double-space the printout.

Lines 1770 through 1890 send the second video line to the printer and print one carriage return when done.

Lines 1900 through 2010 print -'s across the page and finish with a carriage return.

Lines 2020 through 2070 set up the starting and ending addresses by using the contents of STABUF and ENDBUF. They also establish the number of locations to print out by subtracting the ending address from the starting address and storing the remainder in TOTBUF. DE is then loaded with the starting address, and BC is loaded with the total number of bytes to be sent.

Lines 2080 through 2380 are the START routine. The data is converted in the HEXCV routine and sent to the printer by first loading the A register with the D register, then converting that value and printing it. Next the A register is loaded with the E register and the process is repeated. Finally the A register is loaded with the contents of DE, and the process is repeated one last time. At the end of the entire pass, the BC register pair is POPPed back and decremented. If this causes the value of BC to be zero, then the program will return to 5000H for the next locations that you may want to run. If not, then the start routine is repeated.

Line 2390 starts the SCAN routine. The A register is loaded with a # sign and it is printed on the screen. Then the DE register pair is saved and the ROM-based SCAN routine is called. Then the DE register pair is POPPed back. After this is done the contents of the A register which has the value of the key pressed during the SCAN routine, is checked against each of the possible hex digits 0 through F. If a true comparison is found, the B register is loaded with the decimal value represented by the character, and the program returns to the main routine. If no comparison is found, the routine continues to the next test, until it has tested for the F. If it does not return a true on the F, the SCAN routine is repeated.

Lines 3080 through 3240 convert the value stored in the location contained in the A register to its ASCII value for printing. In this routine, the C register is used to hold the original value in the A register. Then the value in the A register is shifted left four times and a test is performed to see if the character in the A register is a valid hex number. In the TEST portion, the character has 30H added to it to provide the ASCII value. Then it is tested to see if it is 9 or less. If it is, the H register is loaded with the value, and the process is repeated by loading the A register with the C register and tested again. After the TEST has been completed, the L register is loaded with the value in A and the HL register pair will contain the 2 ASCII values. In the event that a test proves to be greater than 9, then 7 is added to the A register to produce the value of the letter.

Lines 3250 through 3350 are the POUT or print out routine. Here the character is sent to the printer in the same way as was done in earlier examples. The time delay loop in lines 3320 through 3340 enables us to send more than one piece of data at a time.

Lines 3360 through 3380 set the buffer areas by DEFining Space (DEFS) for them of 2 bytes each. The reason we used 2 locations was that the values stored in these buffers would seldom be less than 255 or FFH.

Lines 3390 and 3400 are the messages, each of which was entered at a length of 20 characters (spaces were added to make them even and provide for tabbing).

Lines 3410 through 3440 set the values of the tables by DEFW (Define Word). These values are the multipliers in the add routines above.

Line 3450 is the mandatory END statement.

TPXFER

This program (Fig. 18-10) will permit you to copy a system tape as long as it doesn't have a boot loader on it. It works on Model I and III TRS-80 systems. The ORG can be changed if desired, but if it is the buffer will become smaller.

You should key in this one, and keep it handy. I had several tapes that I was worried about losing, so I wrote it to save them by making copies. I then used the copies and filed the original tapes away safe and sound.

I have also found cases where a system tape wouldn't load into a machine. By making a copy of the tape with TPXFER, I was able to produce a working copy of the tape even though the original wouldn't work. A system tape follows the format: shown in Fig. 18-11.

The process is simple. The machine listens to the tape until it hears (if you will) a 55H file header. It then looks for the next 6 bytes which are the file name. That's how it knows whether its loading in the right program. The next thing that it looks for is a 3CH data header. That tells it that it is going to get data next.

```
5000              00100          ORG     5000H
5000 CDC901       00110 START    CALL    01C9H
5003 11193C       00120          LD      DE.3C00H+25
5006 213753       00130          LD      HL.MESS1
5009 010B00       00140          LD      BC.MESS1L
500C EDB0         00150          LDIR
500E 11803D       00160 ML1A     LD      DE.3C00H+384
5011 214253       00170          LD      HL.MESS2
5014 011000       00180          LD      BC.MESS2L
5017 EDB0         00190          LDIR
5019 11003E       00200          LD      DE.3C00H+512
501C 215253       00210          LD      HL.MESS3
501F 012200       00220          LD      BC.MESS3L
5022 EDB0         00230          LDIR
5024 11403E       00240          LD      DE.3C00H+576
5027 217453       00250          LD      HL.MESS4
502A 012100       00260          LD      BC,MESS4L
502D EDB0         00270          LDIR
502F 11803E       00280          LD      DE.3C00H+640
5032 219553       00290          LD      HL,MESS5
5035 011900       00300          LD      BC,MESS5L
5038 EDB0         00310          LDIR
503A 11C03E       00320          LD      DE,3C00H+704
503D 21AE53       00330          LD      HL,MESS6
5040 012800       00340          LD      BC,MESS6L
5043 EDB0         00350          LDIR
                  00360 ;
                  00370 ;        TURN CURSOR OFF
                  00380 ;
5045 3E0F         00390          LD      A,0FH
5047 D5           00400          PUSH    DE
5048 FDE5         00410          PUSH    IY
504A CD3300       00420          CALL    033H
504D FDE1         00430          POP     IY
                  00440 ;
                  00450 ;        SCAN KEYBOARD FOR FUNCTION REQUEST
                  00460 ;
504F CD4900       00470 SCAN     CALL    049H
5052 FE4C         00480          CP      'L'
5054 CA6850       00490          JP      Z,LOAD
5057 FE53         00500          CP      'S'
5059 CA3351       00510          JP      Z,SAVE
505C FE56         00520          CP      'V'
505E CA8A51       00530          JP      Z,VERR
5061 FE45         00540          CP      'E'
5063 CAE751       00550          JP      Z,QUIT
5066 18E7         00560          JR      SCAN
                  00570 ;
                  00580 ;        LOAD IN A PROGRAM HERE
                  00590 ;
5068 CDC901       00600 LOAD     CALL    01C9H
506B 210000       00610          LD      HL,0000
506E 22FF54       00620          LD      (T1BUF),HL
5071 110A3C       00630          LD      DE,3C00H+10
5074 21F152       00640          LD      HL,LMES1
5077 012F00       00650          LD      BC,LDMS1L
507A EDB0         00660          LDIR
507C CDFB51       00670          CALL    BREAK
507F CDC901       00680          CALL    01C9H
5082 11003C       00690          LD      DE,3C00H
5085 212053       00700          LD      HL.LDMS2
5088 010C00       00710          LD      BC.LDMS2L
508B EDB0         00720          LDIR
508D 3E00         00730          LD      A.0000
508F 32F954       00740          LD      (BITBUF).A
5092 32FA54       00750          LD      (BITBUF+1).A
5095 210000       00760          LD      HL.0000
5098 110355       00770          LD      DE.TXTBUF
509B 3E00         00780          LD      A.0
509D CD1202       00790          CALL    0212H
50A0 CD9602       00800          CALL    0296H
50A3 CD3502       00810          CALL    0235H
                  00820 ;
```

Fig. 18-10. Copy Systems Tapes with This Routine.

```
                    ;       GET & CHECK FILE HEADER
                    ;
50A6 12                     LD      (DE),A
50A7 13                     INC     DE
50A8 23                     INC     HL
50A9 FE55                   CP      55H
50AB C21F51                 JP      NZ,BADLD
                    ;
                    ;       GET FILE NAME
                    ;
50AE 0606                   LD      B,6
50B0 CD3502         LL2     CALL    0235H
50B3 12                     LD      (DE),A
50B4 13                     INC     DE
50B5 23                     INC     HL
50B6 10F8                   DJNZ    LL2
                    ;
                    ;       CHECK DATA HEADER
                    ;
50B8 CD3502                 CALL    0235H
50BB FE3C                   CP      3CH
50BD C21F51                 JP      NZ,BADLD
50C0 12                     LD      (DE),A
50C1 13                     INC     DE
50C2 23                     INC     HL
                    ;
                    ;       GET BYTE COUNT
                    ;
50C3 CD3502         LL3     CALL    0235H
50C6 32F954                 LD      (BITBUF),A
50C9 12                     LD      (DE),A
50CA 13                     INC     DE
50CB 23                     INC     HL
                    ;
                    ;       GET STARTING ADDRESS
                    ;
50CC 0602                   LD      B,2
50CE CD3502         LL4     CALL    0235H
50D1 12                     LD      (DE),A
50D2 13                     INC     DE
50D3 23                     INC     HL
50D4 10F8                   DJNZ    LL4
                    ;
                    ;       READ DATA
                    ;
50D6 3AF954                 LD      A,(BITBUF)
50D9 47                     LD      B,A
50DA CD3502         LL5     CALL    0235H
50DD 12                     LD      (DE),A
50DE 13                     INC     DE
50DF 23                     INC     HL
50E0 CDD252                 CALL    TOTAL
50E3 10F5                   DJNZ    LL5
                    ;
                    ;       GET CHECKSUM
                    ;
50E5 CD3502                 CALL    0235H
50E8 12                     LD      (DE),A
50E9 13                     INC     DE
50EA 23                     INC     HL
                    ;
                    ;       READ NEXT HEADER
                    ;
50EB CDBE52                 CALL    BLINK
50EE CD3502                 CALL    0235H
50F1 12                     LD      (DE),A
50F2 13                     INC     DE
50F3 23                     INC     HL
50F4 FE3C                   CP      3CH
50F6 CAC350                 JP      Z,LL3
50F9 FE78                   CP      78H
50FB C21F51                 JP      NZ,BADLD
                    ;
```

Fig. 18-10. Continued from page 151.

```
                ;       GET ENTRY ADDRESS
                ;
5ØFE Ø6Ø2                LD      B,2
51ØØ CD35Ø2      LL6     CALL    Ø235H
51Ø3 12                  LD      (DE),A
51Ø4 13                  INC     DE
51Ø5 23                  INC     HL
51Ø6 1ØF8                DJNZ    LL6
51Ø8 22F954              LD      (BITBUF),HL
51ØB CDF8Ø1              CALL    Ø1F8H
51ØE CDC9Ø1              CALL    Ø1C9H
5111 11143C              LD      DE,3CØØH+2Ø
5114 212C53              LD      HL,LDMS3
5117 Ø1ØBØØ              LD      BC,LDMS3L
511A EDBØ                LDIR
511C C31652              JP      BL2
                ;
                ;       BAD LOAD
                ;
511F CDF8Ø1      BADLD   CALL    Ø1F8H
5122 CDC9Ø1              CALL    Ø1C9H
5125 11193C              LD      DE,3CØØH+25
5128 21EØ52              LD      HL,BADM1
512B Ø111ØØ              LD      BC,BADM1L
512E EDBØ                LDIR
513Ø C31652              JP      BL2
                ;
                ;       RE-WRITE THE PROGRAM TO NEW TAPE HERE
                ;
5133 CDC9Ø1      SAVE    CALL    Ø1C9H
5136 11ØØ3C              LD      DE,3CØØH
5139 216454              LD      HL,SAVMS3
513C Ø11DØØ              LD      BC,SAVM3L
513F EDBØ                LDIR
5141 118A3C              LD      DE,3CØØH+128+1Ø
5144 212Ø54              LD      HL,VERMS4
5147 Ø11CØØ              LD      BC,VERM4L
514A EDBØ                LDIR
514C CDFB51              CALL    BREAK
514F CDC9Ø1              CALL    Ø1C9H
5152 11143C              LD      DE,3CØØH+2Ø
5155 213C54              LD      HL,SAVMS1
5158 Ø1ØFØØ              LD      BC,SAVM1L
515B EDBØ                LDIR
515D 3EØØ                LD      A,Ø
515F CD12Ø2              CALL    Ø212H
5162 CD87Ø2              CALL    Ø287H
5165 ED4BF954            LD      BC,(BITBUF)
5169 11Ø355              LD      DE,TXTBUF
516C 1A          SL2     LD      A,(DE)
516D CD64Ø2              CALL    Ø264H
517Ø 13                  INC     DE
5171 ØB                  DEC     BC
5172 78                  LD      A,B
5173 B1                  OR      C
5174 2ØF6                JR      NZ,SL2
5176 CDF8Ø1              CALL    Ø1F8H
5179 CDC9Ø1              CALL    Ø1C9H
517C 11ØØ3C              LD      DE,3CØØH
517F 214B54              LD      HL,SAVMS2
5182 Ø119ØØ              LD      BC,SAVM2L
5185 EDBØ                LDIR
5187 C31652              JP      BL2
                ;
                ;       VERIFY LOAD HERE
                ;
518A CDC9Ø1      VERR    CALL    Ø1C9H
518D 11143C              LD      DE,3CØØH+2Ø
519Ø 21D653              LD      HL,VERMS1
5193 Ø126ØØ              LD      BC,VERM1L
5196 EDBØ                LDIR
5198 118A3C              LD      DE,3CØØH+128+1Ø
519B 212Ø54              LD      HL,VERMS4
519E Ø11CØØ              LD      BC,VERM4L
```

```
51A1 EDB0                LDIR
51A3 CDFB51              CALL    BREAK
51A6 CDC901              CALL    01C9H
51A9 11143C              LD      DE,3C00H+20
51AC 21FC53              LD      HL,VERMS2
51AF 010F00              LD      BC,VERM2L
51B2 EDB0                LDIR
51B4 ED4BF954            LD      BC,(BITBUF)
51B8 210355              LD      HL,TXTBUF
51BB CD1202              CALL    0212H
51BE CD9602              CALL    0296H
51C1 CD3502     VL2      CALL    0235H
51C4 BE                  CP      (HL)
51C5 C21F51              JP      NZ,BADLD
51C8 FE3C                CP      3CH
51CA CCBE52              CALL    Z,BLINK
51CD 23                  INC     HL
51CE 0B                  DEC     BC
51CF 78                  LD      A,B
51D0 B1                  OR      C
51D1 20EE                JR      NZ,VL2
51D3 CDF801              CALL    01F8H
51D6 CDC901              CALL    01C9H
51D9 11193C              LD      DE,3C00H+25
51DC 210B54              LD      HL,VERMS3
51DF 011500              LD      BC,VERM3L
51E2 EDB0                LDIR
51E4 C31652              JP      BL2
                ;
                ;        RETURN TO READY STATE
                ;
51E7 CDC901     QUIT     CALL    01C9H
51EA 110A3C              LD      DE,3C00H+10
51ED 21D554              LD      HL,QUIT1
51F0 012400              LD      BC,QUIT1L
51F3 EDB0                LDIR
51F5 CDFB51              CALL    BREAK
51F8 C3191A     LOOP     JP      1A19H
                ;
                ;        BREAK FOR SAFETY MEASURES HERE
                ;
51FB 11803D     BREAK    LD      DE,3C00H+256+128
51FE 218154              LD      HL,BRKMS
5201 012000              LD      BC,BRKMS1
5204 EDB0                LDIR
5206 CD4900     BL1      CALL    049H
5209 FE0D                CP      0DH
520B C8                  RET     Z
520C FE4D                CP      'M'
520E 20F6                JR      NZ,BL1
5210 CDC901              CALL    01C9H
5213 C30E50              JP      ML1A
5216 ED5B0C55   BL2      LD      DE,(HLDBUF)
521A ED53FB54            LD      (STABUF),DE
521E 2AFB54              LD      HL,(STABUF)
5221 ED5BFF54            LD      DE,(T1BUF)
5225 19                  ADD     HL,DE
5226 22FD54              LD      (ENDBUF),HL
5229 ED4BF954            LD      BC,(BITBUF)
522D 210355              LD      HL,TXTBUF
5230 23         EL1      INC     HL
5231 0B                  DEC     BC
5232 78                  LD      A,B
5233 B1                  OR      C
5234 20FA                JR      NZ,EL1
5236 2B                  DEC     HL
5237 2B                  DEC     HL
5238 7E                  LD      A,(HL)
5239 320155              LD      (ENTBUF),A
523C 23                  INC     HL
523D 7E                  LD      A,(HL)
523E 320255              LD      (ENTBUF+1),A
5241 118F3C              LD      DE,3C00H+143
5244 21A154              LD      HL,SCMS1
```

Fig. 18-10. Continued from page 153.

```
5247 010F00   03040         LD      BC,SCMS1L
524A EDB0     03050         LDIR
524C 210455   03060         LD      HL,TXTBUF+1
524F 010600   03070         LD      BC,6
5252 EDB0     03080         LDIR
5254 11003D   03090         LD      DE,3C00H+256
5257 21B054   03100         LD      HL,SCMS2
525A 010900   03110         LD      BC,SCMS2L
525D EDB0     03120         LDIR
525F 2AFB54   03130         LD      HL,(STABUF)
5262 CD8452   03140         CALL    LP2
5265 21B954   03150         LD      HL,SCMS3
5268 010D00   03160         LD      BC,SCMS3L
526B EDB0     03170         LDIR
526D 2AFD54   03180         LD      HL,(ENDBUF)
5270 CD8452   03190         CALL    LP2
5273 21C654   03200         LD      HL,SCMS4
5276 010F00   03210         LD      BC,SCMS4L
5279 EDB0     03220         LDIR
527B 2A0155   03230         LD      HL,(ENTBUF)
527E CD8452   03240         CALL    LP2
5281 C30E50   03250         JP      ML1A
5284 7C       03260 LP2     LD      A,H
5285 E5       03270         PUSH    HL
5286 CD9852   03280         CALL    CONV
5289 CDB752   03290         CALL    PRNT
528C E1       03300         POP     HL
528D 7D       03310         LD      A,L
528E CD9852   03320         CALL    CONV
5291 CDB752   03330         CALL    PRNT
5294 13       03340         INC     DE
5295 13       03350         INC     DE
5296 13       03360         INC     DE
5297 C9       03370         RET
              03380 ;
              03390 ;       CONVERT TO ASCII HERE
              03400 ;
5298 4F       03410 CONV    LD      C,A
5299 CB3F     03420         SRL     A
529B CB3F     03430         SRL     A
529D CB3F     03440         SRL     A
529F CB3F     03450         SRL     A
52A1 CDAD52   03460         CALL    CT1
52A4 67       03470         LD      H,A
52A5 79       03480         LD      A,C
52A6 E60F     03490         AND     0FH
52A8 CDAD52   03500         CALL    CT1
52AB 6F       03510         LD      L,A
52AC C9       03520         RET
52AD C630     03530 CT1     ADD     A,30H
52AF FE3A     03540         CP      3AH
52B1 FAB652   03550         JP      M,LP9
52B4 C607     03560         ADD     A,7
52B6 C9       03570 LP9     RET
              03580 ;
              03590 ;       PRINT CHARACTER ON SCREEN HERE
              03600 ;
52B7 7C       03610 PRNT    LD      A,H
52B8 12       03620         LD      (DE),A
52B9 13       03630         INC     DE
52BA 7D       03640         LD      A,L
52BB 12       03650         LD      (DE),A
52BC 13       03660         INC     DE
52BD C9       03670         RET
              03680 ;
              03690 ;       BLINK * HERE
              03700 ;
              03710 ;
              03720 ;       TO USE ON A MODEL III, RE WRITE THE
                            ROUTINE AT
              03730 ;       BLINK TO LOOK LIKE THIS:        BLINK   RET
              03740 ;
52BE 3A3F3C   03750 BLINK   LD      A,(3C00H+63)
```

```
52C1 FE2A       Ø376Ø            CP       2AH
52C3 CACC52     Ø377Ø            JP       Z,AOFF
52C6 3E2A       Ø378Ø            LD       A,2AH
52C8 323F3C     Ø379Ø            LD       (3CØØH+63),A
52CB C9         Ø38ØØ            RET
                Ø381Ø ;
                Ø382Ø ;          TURN * OFF HERE
                Ø383Ø ;
52CC 3E2Ø       Ø384Ø AOFF       LD       A,2ØH
52CE 323F3C     Ø385Ø            LD       (3CØØH+63),A
52D1 C9         Ø386Ø            RET
                Ø387Ø ;
                Ø388Ø ;CALCULATE TOTAL # OF BYTES HERE
                Ø389Ø ;
52D2 C5         Ø39ØØ TOTAL      PUSH     BC
52D3 D5         Ø391Ø            PUSH     DE
52D4 E5         Ø392Ø            PUSH     HL
52D5 2AFF54     Ø393Ø            LD       HL,(T1BUF)
52D8 23         Ø394Ø            INC      HL
52D9 22FF54     Ø395Ø            LD       (T1BUF),HL
52DC E1         Ø396Ø            POP      HL
52DD D1         Ø397Ø            POP      DE
52DE C1         Ø398Ø            POP      BC
52DF C9         Ø399Ø            RET
                Ø4ØØØ ;
                Ø4Ø1Ø ;          MESSAGES AND BUFFER ASIGNMENTS HERE
                Ø4Ø2Ø ;
52EØ 42         Ø4Ø3Ø BADM1      DEFM     'BAD CASSETTE LOAD'
     41 44 2Ø 43 41 53 53 45
     54 54 45 2Ø 4C 4F 41 44
ØØ11            Ø4Ø4Ø BADM1L     EQU      $-BADM1
52F1 49         Ø4Ø5Ø LMES1      DEFM     'INCERT TAPE TO BE COPIED,
                                           THEN PRESS  * ENTER *'
     4E 43 45 52 54 2Ø 54 41
     5Ø 45 2Ø 54 4F 2Ø 42 45
     2Ø 43 4F 5Ø 49 45 44 2C
     2Ø 54 48 45 4E 2Ø 5Ø 52
     45 53 53 2Ø 2Ø 2A 2Ø 45
     4E 54 45 52 2Ø 2A
ØØ2F            Ø4Ø6Ø LDMS1L     EQU      $-LMES1
532Ø 4C         Ø4Ø7Ø LDMS2      DEFM     'LOADING TAPE'
     4F 41 44 49 4E 47 2Ø 54
     41 5Ø 45
ØØØC            Ø4Ø8Ø LDMS2L     EQU      $-LDMS2
532C 54         Ø4Ø9Ø LDMS3      DEFM     'TAPE LOADED'
     41 5Ø 45 2Ø 4C 4F 41 44
     45 44
ØØØB            Ø41ØØ LDMS3L     EQU      $-LDMS3
5337 54         Ø411Ø MESS1      DEFM     'TAPE COPIER'
     41 5Ø 45 2Ø 43 4F 5Ø 49
     45 52
ØØØB            Ø412Ø MESS1L     EQU      $-MESS1
5342 45         Ø413Ø MESS2      DEFM     'ENTER          TO'
     4E 54 45 52 2Ø 2Ø 2Ø 2Ø
     2Ø 2Ø 2Ø 2Ø 2Ø 54 4F
ØØ1Ø            Ø414Ø MESS2L     EQU      $-MESS2
5352 2Ø         Ø415Ø MESS3      DEFM     '  L       LOAD PROGRAM TO
                                                     BE COPIED'
     2Ø 4C 2Ø 2Ø 2Ø 2Ø 2Ø 2Ø
     4C 4F 41 44 2Ø 5Ø 52 4F
     47 52 41 4D 2Ø 54 4F 2Ø
     42 45 2Ø 43 4F 5Ø 49 45
     44
ØØ22            Ø416Ø MESS3L     EQU      $-MESS3
5374 2Ø         Ø417Ø MESS4      DEFM     '  S       SAVE PROGRAM ON NEW TAPE'
     2Ø 53 2Ø 2Ø 2Ø 2Ø 2Ø 2Ø
     53 41 56 45 2Ø 5Ø 52 4F
     47 52 41 4D 2Ø 4F 4E 2Ø
     4E 45 57 2Ø 54 41 5Ø 45
ØØ21            Ø418Ø MESS4L     EQU      $-MESS4
5395 2Ø         Ø419Ø MESS5      DEFM     '  V       VERRIFY NEW TAPE'
     2Ø 56 2Ø 2Ø 2Ø 2Ø 2Ø 2Ø
     56 45 52 52 49 46 59 2Ø
```

Fig. 18-10. Continued from page 155.

```
     4E 45 57 20 54 41 50 45
0019              04200 MESS5L   EQU      $-MESS5
53AE 20           04210 MESS6    DEFM     '   E     END SESSION AND
                                           RETURN TO BASIC'
     20 45 20 20 20 20 20 20
     45 4E 44 20 53 45 53 53
     49 4F 4E 20 41 4E 44 20
     52 45 54 55 52 4E 20 54
     4F 20 42 41 53 49 43
0028              04220 MESS6L   EQU      $-MESS6
53D6 50           04230 VERMS1   DEFM     'PREPARE RECORDER TO PLAY BACK
                                          NEW TAPE'
     52 45 50 41 52 45 20 52
     45 43 4F 52 44 45 52 20
     54 4F 20 50 4C 41 59 20
     42 41 43 4B 20 4E 45 57
     20 54 41 50 45
0026              04240 VERM1L   EQU      $-VERMS1
53FC 56           04250 VERMS2   DEFM     'VERRIFYING LOAD'
     45 52 52 49 46 59 49 4E
     47 20 4C 4F 41 44
000F              04260 VERM2L   EQU      $-VERMS2
540B 4/           04270 VERMS3   DEFM     'GOOD DUMP TO NEW TAPE'
     4F 4F 44 20 44 55 4D 50
     20 54 4F 20 4E 45 57 20
     54 41 50 45
0015              04280 VERM3L   EQU      $-VERMS3
5420 50           04290 VERMS4   DEFM     'PRESS  * ENTER *  WHEN READY'
     52 45 53 53 20 20 2A 20
     45 4E 54 45 52 20 2A 20
     20 57 48 45 4E 20 52 45
     41 44 59
001C              04300 VERM4L   EQU      $-VERMS4
543C 53           04310 SAVMS1   DEFM     'SAVEING PROGRAM'
     41 56 45 49 4E 47 20 50
     52 4F 47 52 41 4D
000F              04320 SAVM1L   EQU      $-SAVMS1
544B 50           04330 SAVMS2   DEFM     'PROGRAM SAVED ON NEW TAPE'
     52 4F 47 52 41 4D 20 53
     41 56 45 44 20 4F 4E 20
     4E 45 57 20 54 41 50 45
0019              04340 SAVM2L   EQU      $-SAVMS2
5464 50           04350 SAVMS3   DEFM     'PREPARE TO RECORD ON NEW TAPE'
     52 45 50 41 52 45 20 54
     4F 20 52 45 43 4F 52 44
     20 4F 4E 20 4E 45 57 20
     54 41 50 45
001D              04360 SAVM3L   EQU      $-SAVMS3
5481 20           04370 BRKMS    DEFM     '     OR  - -  PRESS  M  FOR MENU'
     20 20 20 20 4F 52 20 20
     2D 20 2D 20 20 50 52 45
     53 53 20 20 4D 20 20 46
     4F 52 20 4D 45 4E 55
0020              04380 BRKMS1   EQU      $-BRKMS
54A1 46           04390 SCMS1    DEFM     'FILE NAME IS    '
     49 4C 45 20 4E 41 4D 45
     20 49 53 20 20 20
000F              04400 SCMS1L   EQU      $-SCMS1
54B0 53           04410 SCMS2    DEFM     'START @  '
     54 41 52 54 20 40 20 20
0009              04420 SCMS2L   EQU      $-SCMS2
54B9 20           04430 SCMS3    DEFM     '      END @  '
     20 20 20 20 20 45 4E 44
     20 40 20 20
000D              04440 SCMS3L   EQU      $-SCMS3
54C6 20           04450 SCMS4    DEFM     '      ENTRY @  '
     20 20 20 20 20 45 4E 54
     52 59 20 40 20 20
000F              04460 SCMS4L   EQU      $-SCMS4
54D5 50           04470 QUIT1    DEFM     'PRESS  * ENTER *  TO RETURN TO
                                          BASIC'
     52 45 53 53 20 20 2A 20
     45 4E 54 45 52 20 2A 20
     20 54 4F 20 52 45 54 55
```

```
        52 4E 20 54 4F 20 42 41
        53 49 43
0024            04480 QUIT1L   EQU      $-QUIT1
0002            04490 BITBUF   DEFS     2
0002            04500 STABUF   DEFS     2
0002            04510 ENDBUF   DEFS     2
0002            04520 T1BUF    DEFS     2
0002            04530 ENTBUF   DEFS     2
5503            04540 TXTBUF   EQU      ENTBUF+2
550C            04550 HLDBUF   EQU      TXTBUF+9
5000            04560          END      START
```

Fig. 18-10. Continued from page 157.

Following the data header is the byte count or the number of bytes in the block that it is going to load. This number can be anywhere from 6 to 255. Not all blocks have 255 bytes in them.

After getting the number of bytes that it will read, it then reads the starting address. This is not necessarily the starting address of the program, but rather the address in memory that the block will start loading into. This is important to remember because some authors have been known to zig zag load their programs, or, load the first block in at 5000H, the second in at 6000H, and the next one in at 5500H. While all of these blocks are used by the program, the author may have used this to make it tougher to decode or copy the program, or it may have been assembled with a special assembler that allows one program to be written from several others.

After the system has loaded in the number of bytes started in the byte counter byte (no confusion meant), it then reads the checksum byte. This byte must match the number of bytes read by the system or else you will get that familiar * C meaning it didn't work, try again.

The next byte that is read in is another header. Here the system has to check to see if it is going to get another data block, 3CH, or see if it has read the last one in the program, 78H.

If it finds a 3CH, then it will go through the process again starting with the byte count. If not, it then looks for the last two bytes or the program entry point. When it gets that address, it then transfers control to it after you type / and hit the enter key.

Now that you know how a system tape is read into the computer, let's look at the transfer program.

Line 100 is the ORG statement. This point can be changed, but the size of the system program that can be copied will be decreased. This program uses an internal buffer to store the data read in from the tape. Any data coming in goes in that buffer and not into the memory address that the tape tells it to.

Lines 110 through 350 clear the screen, and put the menu on the screen.

Lines 390 through 430 turn the cursor off. If you wish to leave it on, delete these lines.

Lines 470 through 560 call the ROM-based keyboard scan routine, and check for the key pressed. If no key was pressed, the routine is repeated. If a valid selection was made, the program branches to the appropriate routine. Invalid keys cause a repeat of the scan routine.

Line 600 starts the LOAD routine. The first thing that it does is to zero out the temporary memory buffer. It then displays a message on the screen that allows you to continue or go back to the menu. This is important as you may have made the wrong selection, and told it to load instead of save or verify. If you did want it to load a program into memory, then the program continues at line 680.

Line 680 through 720 print the load program message.

Lines 730 through 760 zero out the rest of the buffers, and prepare to load the program into memory.

File header	55H	1 byte
File name		6 bytes
Data header	3CH	1 byte
Byte count		1 byte
Starting address		2 bytes
Data		up to 255 bytes
Checksum		1 byte
Entry header	78H	1 byte
Entry address		2 bytes

Fig. 18-11. Systems Tapes Formats.

Line 770 sets the pointer to the bottom of the program text buffer.

Line 780 defines the tape drive to be used.

Line 790 calls the ROM-based routine to find the sync byte on the tape leader.

Line 800 calls the ROM-based routine to read in one byte from the tape.

Lines 840 through 870 increment the pointers and counters and check to see if it was a file header.

Line 880 tells the program that if it was a file header to tell you it was a bad load. At this point it shouldn't have gotten a file header.

Lines 920 through 970 tell the program to load in the next 6 bytes. These are the file name of the tape.

Lines 1010 through 1060 get the next byte and check to see if the data header was there. If it wasn't, then the program tells you that you have a bad load. If it was, the pointers are incremented, and the counters incremented.

Lines 1100 through 1140 read the next byte and position the counters and pointers accordingly.

Lines 1180 through 1230 get the starting address of the block that will be read in. The pointers and counters are then incremented and positioned.

Lines 1270 through 1340 read in the actual data block.

Lines 1380 through 1410 read in the checksum byte.

Lines 1450 through 1530 read in the next header and check to see if it is going to be data or if it is an entry header. If it is a data header, the program returns to LL3, and reads the next block. If it is not a data header or an entry header, the program goes to the bad load routine.

Lines 1570 through 1630 read in the entry address and store it.

Lines 1640 through 1700 turn off the motor, clear the screen, and then jump to BL2.

Lines 1740 through 1800 turn off the motor, clear the screen, and print the BAD LOAD message. The program then jumps to BL2.

Lines 1840 through 1980 clear the screen, display the

messages to save the tape, then call the last chance mode (BREAK).

Lines 1990 through 2170 define the drive, turn the motor on, write the leader on the new tape, then do a bit by bit transfer of data from the memory buffer to the tape. This buffer contains all of the data and headers from the original tape, so we don't need to worry about putting the headers on the new tape.

Lines 2210 through 2350 clear the screen and print the necessary verify tape messages.

Lines 2360 through 2390 set up the buffer pointers and the tape deck for the bit by bit read-verify routine.

Lines 2400 through 2560 read in a byte from the tape. This byte is then compared with the contents of the buffer. If it doesn't match, the program jumps to the bad load routine. If they do match, the pointer is incremented, and the next byte is read in. Notice here that the BC register pair is used to keep track of the number of bytes read in to the verify routine.

Lines 2600 through 2660 are the program exit routine. Here the program gives you the usual chance to get back to the menu. If you choose to end the program, this routine does a jump to 1A19H, the BASIC READY execution point. Disk system users can change this address and have the program return to the DOS READY state. To do this you should look for that address in your DOS operations manual.

Lines 2700 through 2800 are the lines that compose the last chance routine. Here you get the message to confirm the selection. Pressing the ENTER key here will cause the routine to return to the calling routine. Pressing the 'M' key causes the program to return to the main menu. Notice that instead of using the keyboard scan routine located at 02BH, we use the routine at 049H. This routine will not return to the calling routine, in this case the BREAK routine, until a key is pressed. You will also note that only the ENTER key and the M key are valid entries. Any other key will cause the program to go back and look for another key.

Lines 2810 through 2880 are the routine to count the total number of bytes in the program that were read in. This is done by adding the contents of the HLDBUF and the STABUF. A third buffer, STABUF, is used here to maintain the contents of the HLDBUF.

Lines 2890 through 3000 compute the ending address.

Lines 3010 through 3230 display the starting, ending, and entry point address messages and the addresses.

Lines 3240 through 3500 are the hex to ASCII convert routine that we used in HARDBUG. Here they are used to convert the contents of the buffers so that these addresses can be displayed.

Lines 3590 through 3650 constitute a quick and primitive, routine to print the contents of HL on the screen.

Lines 3690 through 3809 contain the routine to blink the * on the upper right hand corner of the screen. I know there is a ROM routine that will do that for you, but let's be a little imaginative here. This routine checks to see if there is an asterisk on the screen. If there is, it prints a space there, if not it prints an asterisk. The asterisk does *not* blink at the end of each block like it does in the ROM routine. Here we have it blink so that we know that the program is doing something while we are waiting. The ROM routine blinks it after each block. You can modify this program to do the same thing yourself. I will give you a hint. All you will have to do is move a line or two or three around. Where to move what is what I want you to figure out. By the way, I know and I won't tell!

Lines 3840 through 3930 list the routine that keeps track of how many bytes are being read.

The rest of the program defines the messages and sets the buffer sizes. Again, I strongly suggest that you place this program in your library and use it. It can save you much grief and money too.

Chapter 19
BASIC to Machine: The Shapes Program

I know that right about now you are saying, "There has to be an easier way." Well there is. Its called a BASIC compiler. It must point out that, as in most things in life, the easy way is not always the best.

A BASIC compiler takes a BASIC program and compiles it into a machine-language program. The principle behind it is that it supposedly places commonly used routines so that they can be used over again. It then compiles the program into a machine code.

There are a few drawbacks though. They are:

1. The compiler itself takes up 12K of memory.
2. You must have a disk system to use it.
3. You cannot compile a program over 4 grans long and to do a 4-gran program, you must have a 48K byte machine.

We will not compile one here, but I will give a demonstration of how to convert a BASIC program to machine language. By the way, I did compile this program to see how long the listing would be.

It took 147 pages of paper to list it. One of the reasons that it is so long is that part of the compiler has to reside within the program to make it work.

This program draws two rectangles and a square on the screen. The square is placed at random in position 1, 2, or 3. I designed this program for a local Head Start school program to teach the children to find the shape that did not belong.

Now, let's convert a program in BASIC to assembly language. The first thing that we must do is have the BASIC program. To do this we must have a plan of what we want the program to do. In this case, we have a client that needs a program that will display three shapes on the screen. Two of these shapes must be the same, and one must be different.

Our client wants to use this as an educational tool. Its purpose is to teach pre-school children the different shapes. Our client also teaches the children to count from 1 to 10.

Keeping the program simple and offering rewards, let's have the computer draw two rectangles and a square. These figures will be numbered, and the square will be placed at random in one of the three figure positions. Each figure will be numbered. This will permit us to teach the first three numbers at the same time. The BASIC version of the program is shown in Fig. 19-1.

Line 10 clears string space, clears the screen, and moves the cursor down 2 lines from the top. It also uses the random generator to get a random number between 1 and 3 into the N variable. It then checks N and depending on what the value of N is, goes to the appropriate pattern routine.

Line 100 prints the numbers 1 through 3 on the screen in the appropriate locations, then calls the routine to print the square and the rectangles on the screen. It then sets the value of J to 1. This tells the computer that the square is in position 1. After it has done all of this, it goes to line 400 where we will check the student's answer. Lines 200 and 300 do the same thing with 200 placing the square in location 2, and 300 placing it in location 3.

Line 400 asks the child which figure is wrong. It then checks to see if the child pressed the right key. If so, the program goes to line 420.

Line 410 tells the child that it was the wrong answer. It also gives the student the right answer then goes to line 430. Line 420 tells the child that he got the right answer. After this

```
10 CLEAR70:CLS:PRINT:PRINT:N=RND(3):ONNGOTO100,200,300
100 PRINTTAB(5)"1"TAB(30)"2"TAB(50)"3":GOSUB1000:
    GOSUB5000:GOSUB6000:J=1:GOTO400
200 PRINTTAB(10)"1"TAB(30)"2"TAB(50)"3":GOSUB4000:
    GOSUB2000:GOSUB6000:J=2:GOTO400
300 PRINTTAB(10)"1"TAB(30)"2"TAB(50)"3":GOSUB4000:
    GOSUB5000:GOSUB3000:J=3
400 PRINT@400,::INPUT"WHICH FIGURE IS WRONG";A:IFA=JTHEN420
410 PRINT@400,::PRINTSTRING$(40," "):PRINT@400,::
    PRINT"WRONG IT WAS ";J:GOTO430
420 PRINT@400,::PRINT"GOOD     YOU GOT IT RIGHT  ":PRINT"
    PRESS THE WHITE KEY TO CONTINUE":GOTO440
430 PRINT"PRESS THE WHITE KEY TO CONTINUE"
440 A$=INKEY$:IFA$=CHR$(13)THENGOTO10ELSE440
1000 FORX=1TO25:SET(X,1):SET(X,10):NEXTX:FORY=1
    TO10:SET(1,Y):SET(25,Y):NEXTY:RETURN
2000 FORX=51TO75:SET(X,1):SET(X,10):NEXTX:FORY=1
    TO10:SET(51,Y):SET(75,Y):NEXTY:RETURN
3000 FORX=85TO110:SET(X,1):SET(X,10):NEXTX:FORY=1
    TO10:SET(85,Y):SET(110,Y):NEXTY:RETURN
4000 FORX=1TO35:SET(X,1):SET(X,10):NEXTX:FORY=1
    TO10:SET(1,Y):SET(35,Y):NEXTY:RETURN
5000 FORX=41TO76:SET(X,1):SET(X,10):NEXTX:FORY=1
    TO10:SET(41,Y):SET(76,Y):NEXTY:RETURN
6000 FORX=86TO121:SET(X,1):SET(X,10):NEXTX:FORY=1
    TO10:SET(86,Y):SET(121,Y):NEXTY:RETURN
```

Fig. 19-1. The Shapes Program in BASIC.

it goes to line 440. Line 430 tells the child to press the white key to continue. Line 440 is an INKEY$ scan routine that checks for the enter key. If not pressed it tries again. If it was pressed, the program starts over again. An interesting note here is that the INKEY$ routine is a call to 02BH, and the CHR$(13) is an ODH or a carriage return!

```
;
;  ORIGIN POINT MAY BE CHANGED IF DESIRED
;
                ORG     8000H
;
;  CLEAR THE SCREEN
;
        START   CALL    01C9H
;
;TOSS THE COIN FOR A NUMBER FROM 1 TO 3
;
        TOSS    LD      A,R         ;GET CONTENTS OF REFRESH REGISTER
                LD      B,A         ;STORE IN THE B REGISTER
                LD      A,R         ;GET IT AGAIN (IT CONTINUALY CHANGES)
                LD      C,A         ;STORE IT IN THE C REGISTER
        DELAY   DEC     BC          ;DELAY TO BE SURE IT'S NOT THE SAME
                LD      A,B
                OR      C
                JR      NZ,DELAY
                LD      A,R         ;NOW IT'S MIXED UP GOOD !!!
                AND     03H         ;MASK IT
                LD      (RND),A
                CP      1
                JP      Z,ONE
                CP      2
                JP      Z,TWO
                CP      3
                JP      Z,THREE
                JP      TOSS        ;IF IT IS MORE TRY AGAIN
        ONE     LD      DE,3C00H+64+10
                LD      A,'1'
                LD      (DE),A
                LD      DE,3C00H+64+29
                LD      A,'2'
                LD      (DE),A
                LD      DE,3C00H+64+51
                LD      A,'3'
                LD      (DE),A
                LD      DE,3C00H+6
                LD      A,140
                LD      BC,10
                CALL    DRAW
                LD      DE,3C00H+192+6
                LD      BC,10
                LD      A,140
                CALL    DRAW
                LD      DE,3C00H+5
                CALL    SIDE1
                LD      DE,3C00H+16
                CALL    SIDE2
                LD      DE,3C00H+21
                LD      BC,17
                LD      A,140
                CALL    DRAW
                LD      DE,3C00H+192+21
                LD      BC,17
```

Fig. 19-2. The Shapes Program in Machine Language.

```
00630                LD      A,140
00640                CALL    DRAW
00650                LD      DE,3C00H+20
00660                CALL    SIDE1
00670                LD      DE,3C00H+20+18
00680                CALL    SIDE2
00690                LD      DE,3C00H+44
00700                LD      BC,17
00710                LD      A,140
00720                CALL    DRAW
00730                LD      DE,3C00H+192+44
00740                LD      BC,17
00750                LD      A,140
00760                CALL    DRAW
00770                LD      DE,3C00H+43
00780                CALL    SIDE1
00790                LD      DE,3C00H+43+17
00800                CALL    SIDE2
00802 ;
00804 ;  SAVE A ONE IN THE RND BUFFER  (IT HAD AN A IN IT)
00806 ;
00810                LD      A,'1'
00820                LD      (RND),A
00830                JP      ANSWER
00840        TWO     LD      DE,3C00H+64+8
00850                LD      A,'1'
00860                LD      (DE),A
00870                LD      DE,3C00H+64+27
00880                LD      A,'2'
00890                LD      (DE),A
00900                LD      DE,3C00H+64+46
00910                LD      A,'3'
00920                LD      (DE),A
00930                LD      DE,3C00H+1
00940                LD      BC,17
00950                LD      A,140
00960                CALL    DRAW
00970                LD      DE,3C00H+192+1
00980                LD      BC,17
00990                LD      A,140
01000                CALL    DRAW
01010                LD      DE,3C00H
01020                CALL    SIDE1
01030                LD      DE,3C00H+18
01040                CALL    SIDE2
01050                LD      DE,3C00H+22+1
01060                LD      BC,10
01070                LD      A,140
01080                CALL    DRAW
01090                LD      DE,3C00H+192+22+1
01100                LD      BC,10
01110                LD      A,140
01120                CALL    DRAW
01130                LD      DE,3C00H+22
01140                CALL    SIDE1
01150                LD      DE,3C00H+22+11
01160                CALL    SIDE2
01170                LD      DE,3C00H+38+1
01180                LD      BC,17
01190                LD      A,140
01200                CALL    DRAW
01210                LD      DE,3C00H+192+38+1
01220                LD      BC,17
```

```
                LD      A,140
                CALL    DRAW
                LD      DE,3C00H+38
                CALL    SIDE1
                LD      DE,3C00H+38+17+1
                CALL    SIDE2
;   STORE A 2 IN RND
;
                LD      A,'2'
                LD      (RND),A
                JP      ANSWER
        THREE   LD      DE,3C00H+64+8
                LD      A,'1'
                LD      (DE),A
                LD      DE,3C00H+64+31
                LD      A,'2'
                LD      (DE),A
                LD      DE,3C00H+64+51
                LD      A,'3'
                LD      (DE),A
                LD      DE,3C00H+1
                LD      BC,17
                LD      A,140
                CALL    DRAW
                LD      DE,3C00H+192+1
                LD      BC,17
                LD      A,140
                CALL    DRAW
                LD      DE,3C00H
                CALL    SIDE1
                LD      DE,3C00H+18
                CALL    SIDE2
;
;   STORE A THREE IN RND
;
                LD      A,'3'
                LD      (RND),A
                LD      DE,3C00H+18+5+1
                LD      A,140
                LD      BC,17
                CALL    DRAW
                LD      DE,3C00H+192+18+5+
                LD      BC,17
                LD      A,140
                CALL    DRAW
                LD      DE,3C00H+18+5
                CALL    SIDE1
                LD      DE,3C00H+18+5+18
                CALL    SIDE2
                LD      DE,3C00H+46+1
                LD      BC,10
                LD      A,140
                CALL    DRAW
                LD      DE,3C00H+192+46+1
                LD      BC,10
                LD      A,140
                CALL    DRAW
                LD      DE,3C00H+46
                CALL    SIDE1
                LD      DE,3C00H+46+11
                CALL    SIDE2
                JP      ANSWER
```

Fig. 19-2. Continued from page 167.

```
;
;   THIS DRAWS THE TOPS AND BOTTOMS
;
        DRAW    LD      (TEMP),BC
                LD      (TEMP1),A
        DRAW1   LD      A,(TEMP1)
                LD      (DE),A
                INC     DE
                DEC     BC
                LD      A,B
                OR      C
                JR      NZ,DRAW1
                RET
        TEMP    DEFS    2
;
;   NOW GET AND CHECK THE ANSWER
;
        ANSWER  LD      DE,3C00H+455
                LD      HL,MESS1
                LD      BC,MESS1L
                LDIR
                LD      A,(RND)
                LD      H,A
        ANSL    CALL    02BH
                JR      Z,ANSL
                CP      H
                JR      Z,RIGHT
                JP      WRONG
;
;   YOU DID IT !!!!
;
        RIGHT   CALL    01C9H
                LD      DE,3C00H+70
                LD      HL,MESS2
                LD      BC,MESS2L
                LDIR
                JP      WAIT
;
;   OOPS, YOU GOOFED UP!
;
        WRONG   CALL    01C9H
                LD      DE,3C00H+448
                LD      HL,MESS3
                LD      BC,MESS3L
                LDIR
                INC     DE
                LD      A,(RND)
                LD      (DE),A
                JP      WAIT
        RND     DEFS    2
        TEMP1   DEFS    2
;
;   DRAW THE LEFT SIDE OF THE FIGURES
;
        SIDE1   LD      A,168
                LD      (DE),A
                CALL    UP64
                LD      A,170
                LD      (DE),A
                CALL    UP64
                LD      (DE),A
                CALL    UP64
                LD      A,138
```

```
02280                 LD      (DE),A
02290                 RET
02292 ;
02294 ;  DRAW THE RIGHT SIDE OF THE FIGURES
02296 ;
02300         SIDE2   LD      A,148
02310                 LD      (DE),A
02320                 CALL    UP64
02330                 LD      A,149
02340                 LD      (DE),A
02350                 CALL    UP64
02360                 LD      (DE),A
02370                 CALL    UP64
02380                 LD      A,133
02390                 LD      (DE),A
02400                 RET
02402 ;
02404 ;  INCREMENT DE 64 TIMES AND PUT IT BELOW WHERE IT IS
NOW
02406 ;
02410         UP64    PUSH    AF
02420                 LD      BC,64
02430         UP64A   INC     DE
02440                 DEC     BC
02450                 LD      A,B
02460                 OR      C
02470                 JR      NZ,UP64A
02480                 POP     AF
02490                 RET
02492 ;
02494 ;  WAIT FOR THE ENTER KEY TO BE PRESSED
02496 ;
02500         WAIT    LD      DE,3C00H+650
02510                 LD      HL,MESS4
02520                 LD      BC,MESS4L
02530                 LDIR
02540         WAIT1   CALL    02BH
02550                 CP      0DH
02560                 JR      NZ,WAIT1
02570                 JP      START
02580         MESS1   DEFM    'WHICH FIGURE IS WRONG?'
02590         MESS1L  EQU     $-MESS1
02600         MESS2   DEFM    'G O O D   YOU  GOT  IT
RIGHT'
02610         MESS2L  EQU     $-MESS2
02620         MESS3   DEFM    'SORRY, WRONG ANSWER,  IT
WAS ..
02630         MESS3L  EQU     $-MESS3
02640         MESS4   DEFM    'PLEASE PRESS THE WHITE KEY
TO TRY ANOTHER ONE'
02650         MESS4L  EQU     $-MESS4
02660                 END     START
```

Fig. 19-2. Continued from page 169.

Line 1000 draws a square in location 1.
Line 2000 draws a square in location 1.
Line 3000 draws a square in location 3.
Line 4000 draws a rectangle in location 1.

Line 5000 draws a rectangle in location 2.
Line 6000 draws a rectangle in location 3.

There you have it. A simple BASIC program to fill our client's needs. Now, let's convert it to machine language. The principle is the same. We follow the same needs of the customer, and for the most part, we can follow the same program flow. It is given in Fig. 19-2.

Appendix A Codes

HEX CONTROL AND KEY CODES

CODE	FUNCTION	CODE	FUNCTION
00H	NONE	10H	NONE
01H	NONE	11H	NONE
02H	NONE	12H	NONE
03H	NONE	13H	NONE
04H	NONE	14H	NONE
05H	NONE	15H	NONE
06H	NONE	16H	NONE
07H	NONE	17H	32 CHAR MODE
08H	BACK SPACE	18H	BACK SPACE
09H	NONE	19H	ADVANCE CURSOR
0AH	LINE FEED WITH CR.	1AH	DOWN FEED
0BH	TOP OF FORM	1BH	UP FEED
0CH	TOP OF FORM	1CH	RETURN TO 3C00H
0DH	CARRIAGE RETURN	1DH	MOVE TO START OF LINE
0EH	TURN CURSOR ON	1EH	ERASE TO END OF LINE
0FH	TURN CURSOR OFF	1FH	CLEAR TO END OF FRAME

CHARACTER CODES

HEX	CHARACTER	HEX	CHARACTER
20H	SPACE	40H	@
21H	!	41H	A
22H	"	42H	B
23H	#	43H	C
24H	$	44H	D
25H	%	45H	E
26H	&	46H	F
27H	'	47H	G
28H	(	48H	H
29H	)	49H	I
2AH	*	4AH	J
2BH	+	4BH	K
2CH	,	4CH	L
2DH	-	4DH	M
2EH	.	4EH	N
2FH	/	4FH	O
30H	0	50H	P
31H	1	51H	Q
32H	2	52H	R
33H	3	53H	S
34H	4	54H	T
35H	5	55H	U
36H	6	56H	V
37H	7	57H	W
38H	8	58H	X
39H	9	59H	Y
3AH	:	5AH	X
3BH	;	5BH	UP ARROW
3CH	<	5CH	DOWN ARROW
3DH	=	5DH	LEFT ARROW
3EH	>	5EH	RIGHT ARROW
3FH	?	5FH	-

LOWERCASE CODES

60H	@	70H	p
61H	a	71H	q
62H	b	72H	r
63H	c	73H	s
64H	d	74H	t
65H	e	75H	u
66H	f	76H	v
67H	g	77H	w
68H	h	78H	x
69H	i	79H	y
6AH	j	7AH	z
6BH	k	7BH	NONE
6CH	l	7CH	NONE
6DH	m	7DH	NONE
6EH	n	7EH	NONE
6FH	o	7FH	NONE

Appendix B JR Suffixes

DISPLACEMENT BACK FROM END OF COMMAND

JR	DISP.	JR	DISP.	JR	DISP.
FE	1	CF	48	A0	95
FD	2	CE	49	9F	96
FC	3	CD	50	9E	97
FB	4	CC	51	9D	98
FA	5	CB	52	9C	99
F9	6	CA	53	9B	100
F8	7	C9	54	9A	101
F7	8	C8	55	99	102
F6	9	C7	56	98	103
F5	10	C6	57	97	104
F4	11	C5	58	96	105
F3	12	C4	59	95	106
F2	13	C3	60	94	107
F1	14	C2	61	93	108
F0	15	C1	62	92	109
EF	16	C0	63	91	110
EE	17	BF	64	90	111
ED	18	BE	65	8F	112
EC	19	BD	66	8E	113
EB	20	BC	67	8D	114
EA	21	BB	68	8C	115
E9	22	BA	69	8B	116
E8	23	B9	70	8A	117
E7	24	B8	71	89	118
E6	25	B7	72	88	119
E5	26	B6	73	87	120
E4	27	B5	74	86	121
E3	28	B4	75	85	122
E2	29	B3	76	84	123
E1	30	B2	77	83	124
E0	31	B1	78	82	125
DF	32	B0	79	81	126
DE	33	AF	80		
DD	34	AE	81		
DC	35	AD	82		
DB	36	AC	83		
DA	37	AB	84		
D9	38	AA	85		
D8	39	A9	86		
D7	40	A8	87		
D6	41	A7	88		
D5	42	A6	89		
D4	43	A5	90		
D3	44	A4	91		
D2	45	A3	92		
D1	46	A2	93		
D0	47	A1	94		

DISPLACEMENT AHEAD OF COMMAND

JR	DISP.	JR	DISP.	JR	DISP.
00	0	30	48	60	96
01	1	31	49	61	97
02	2	32	50	62	98
03	3	33	51	63	99
04	4	34	52	64	100
05	5	35	53	65	101
06	6	36	54	66	102
07	7	37	55	67	103
08	8	38	56	68	104
09	9	39	57	69	105
0A	10	3A	58	6A	106
0B	11	3B	59	6B	107
0C	12	3C	60	6C	108
0D	13	3D	61	6D	109
0E	14	3E	62	6E	110
0F	15	3F	63	6F	111
10	16	40	64	70	112
11	17	41	65	71	113
12	18	42	66	72	114
13	19	43	67	73	115
14	20	44	68	74	116
15	21	45	69	75	117
16	22	46	70	76	118
17	23	47	71	77	119
18	24	48	72	78	120
19	25	49	73	79	121
1A	26	4A	74	7A	122
1B	27	4B	75	7B	123
1C	28	4C	76	7C	124
1D	29	4D	77	7D	125
1E	30	4E	78	7E	126
1F	31	4F	79	7F	127
20	32	50	80	80	128
21	33	51	81		
22	34	52	82		
23	35	53	83		
24	36	54	84		
25	37	55	85		
26	38	56	86		
27	39	57	87		
28	40	58	88		
29	41	59	89		
2A	42	5A	90		
2B	43	5B	91		
2C	44	5C	92		
2D	45	5D	93		
2E	46	5E	94		
2F	47	5F	95		

Appendix C
Numeric List of Machine Codes

MACHINE CODE	COMMAND	MACHINE CODE	COMMAND
00	NOP	35	DEC (HL)
018405	LD (BC),NN	3620	LD (HL),N
02	LD (BC),A	37	SCF
03	INC BC	382E	JR C,DIS
04	INC B	39	ADD HL,SP
05	DEC B	3A8405	LD A,(NN)
0620	LD B,N	3B	DEC SP
07	RLC	3C	INC A
08	EX AF,AF'	3D	DEC A
09	ADD HL,BC	3E20	LD A,N
0A	LD A,(BC)	3F	CCF
0B	DEC B	40	LD B,B
0C	INC C	41	LD B,C
0D	DEC C	42	LD B,D
0E20	LD C,N	43	LD B,E
0F	RRCA	44	LD B,H
102E	DJNZ DIS	45	LD B,L
118405	LD DE,NN	46	LD B,(HL)
12	LD (DE),A	47	LD B,A
13	INC DE	48	LD C,B
14	INC D	49	LD C,C
15	DEC D	4A	LD C,D
1620	LD D,D	4B	LD C,E
17	RLA	4C	LD C,H
182E	JR DIS	4D	LD C,L
19	ADD HL,DE	4E	LD C,(HL)
1A	LD A,(DE)	4F	LD C,A
1B	DEC DE	50	LD D,B
1C	INC E	51	LD D,C
1D	DEC E	52	LD D,D
1E20	LD E,N	53	LD D,E
1F	RRA	54	LD D,H
202E	JR NZ,DIS	55	LD D,L
218405	LD HL,NN	56	LD D,(HL)
228405	LD (NN),HL	57	LD D,A
23	INC HL	58	LD E,B
24	INC H	59	LD E,C
25	DEC H	5A	LD E,D
2620	LD H,N	5B	LD E,E
27	DAA	5C	LD E,H
282E	JR Z,DIS	5D	LD E,L
29	ADD HL,(NN)	5E	LD E,(HL)
2A8405	LD HL,(NN)	5F	LD E,A
2B	DEC HL	60	LD H,B
2C	INC L	61	LD H,C
2D	DEC L	62	LD H,D
2E20	LD L,N	63	LD H,E
2F	CPL	64	LD H,H
302E	JR NC,DIS	65	LD H,L

MACHINE CODE	COMMAND	MACHINE CODE	COMMAND
318405	LD SP,NN	66	LD H,(HL)
328405	LD (NN),A	67	LD H,A
33	INC SP	68	LD L,B
34	INC (HL)	69	LD L,C
6A	LD L,D	9F	SBC A,A
6B	LD L,E	A0	AND B
6C	LD L,H	A1	AND C
6D	LD L,L	A2	AND D
6E	LD L,(HL)	A3	AND E
6F	LD L,A	A4	AND H
70	LD (HL),B	A5	AND L
71	LD (HL),C	A6	AND (HL)
72	LD (HL),D	A7	AND A
73	LD (HL),E	A8	XOR B
74	LD (HL),H	A9	XOR C
75	LD (HL),L	AA	XOR D
76	HALT	AB	XOR E
77	LD (HL),A	AC	XOR H
78	LD A,B	AD	XOR L
79	LD A,C	AE	XOR (HL)
7A	LD A,D	AF	XOR A
7B	LD A,E	B0	OR B
7C	LD A,H	B1	OR C
7D	LD A,L	B2	OR D
7E	LD A,(HL)	B3	OR E
7F	LD A,A	B4	OR H
80	ADD A,B	B5	OR L
81	ADD A,C	B6	OR (HL)
82	ADD A,D	B7	OR A
83	ADD A,E	B8	CP B
84	ADD A,H	B9	CP C
85	ADD A,L	BA	CP D
86	ADD A,(HL)	BB	CP E
87	ADD A,A	BC	CP H
88	ADC A,B	BD	CP L
89	ADC A,C	BE	CP (HL)
8A	ADC A,D	BF	CP A
8B	ADC A,E	C0	RET NZ
8C	ADC A,H	C1	POP BC
8D	ADC A,L	C28405	JP NZ,NN
8E	ADC A,(HL)	C38405	JP NN
8F	ADC A	C48405	CALL NZ,NN
90	SUB B	C5	PUSH BC
91	SUB C	C620	ADD A,N
92	SUB D	C7	RST 0
93	SUB E	C8	RET Z
94	SUB H	C9	RET
95	SUB L	CA8405	JP Z,NN
96	SUB (HL)	CC8405	CALL Z,NN
97	SUB A,B	CD8405	CALL NN
98	SBC A,B	CE20	ADC A,N
99	SBC A,C	CF	RST 8
9A	SBC A,D	D0	RET NC
9B	SBC A,E	D1	POP DE
9C	SBC A,H	D28405	JP NC,NN
9D	SBC A,L	D320	OUT N,A
9E	SBC A,(HL)	D48405	CALL NC,CC

MACHINE CODE	COMMAND	MACHINE CODE	COMMAND
CB4A	BIT 1,D	CB7F	BIT 7,A
CB4B	BIT 1,E	CB80	RES 0,B
CB4C	BIT 1,H	CB81	RES 0,C
CB4D	BIT 1,L	CB82	RES 0,D
CB4E	BIT 1,(HL)	CB83	RES 0,E
CB4F	BIT 1,A	CB84	RES 0,H
CB50	BIT 2,B	CB85	RES 0,L
CB51	BIT 2,C	CB86	RES 0,(HL)
CB52	BIT 2,D	CB87	RES 0,A
CB53	BIT 2,E	CB88	RES 1,B
CB54	BIT 2,H	CB89	RES 1,C
CB55	BIT 2,L	CB8A	RES 1,D
CB56	BIT 2,(HL)	CB8B	RES 1,E
CB57	BIT 2,A	CB8C	RES 1,H
CB58	BIT 3,B	CB8D	RES 1,L
CB59	BIT 3,C	CB8E	RES 1,(HL)
CB5A	BIT 3,D	CB8F	RES 1,A
CB5B	BIT 3,E	CB90	RES 2,B
CB5C	BIT 3,H	CB91	RES 2,C
CB5D	BIT 3,L	CB92	RES 2,D
CB5E	BIT 3,(HL)	CB93	RES 2,E
CB5F	BIT 3,A	CB94	RES 2,H
CB60	BIT 4,B	CB95	RES 2,L
CB61	BIT 4,C	CB96	RES 2,(HL)
CB62	BIT 4,D	CB97	RES 2,A
CB63	BIT 4,E	CB98	RES 3,B
CB64	BIT 4,H	CB99	RES 3,C
CB65	BIT 4,L	CB9A	RES 3,D
CB66	BIT 4,(HL)	CB9B	RES 3,E
CB67	BIT 4,A	CB9C	RES 3,H
CB68	BIT 5,B	CB9D	RES 3,L
CB69	BIT 5,C	CB9E	RES 3,(HL)
CB6A	BIT 5,D	CB9F	RES 3,A
CB6B	BIT 5,E	CBA0	RES 4,B
CB6C	BIT 5,H	CBA1	RES 4,C
CB6D	BIT 5,L	CBA2	RES 4,D
CB6E	BIT 5,(HL)	CBA3	RES 4,E
CB6F	BIT 5,A	CBA4	RES 4,H
CB70	BIT 6,B	CBA5	RES 4,L
CB71	BIT 6,C	CBA6	RES 4,(HL)
CB72	BIT 6,D	CBA7	RES 4,A
CB73	BIT 6,E	CBA8	RES 5,B
CB74	BIT 6,H	CBA9	RES 5,C
CB75	BIT 6,L	CBAA	RES 5,D
CB76	BIT 6,(HL)	CBAB	RES 5,E
CB77	BIT 6,A	CBAC	RES 5,H
CB78	BIT 7,B	CBAD	RES 5,L
CB79	BIT 7,C	CBAE	RES 5,(HL)
CB7A	BIT 7,D	CBAF	RES 5,A
CB7B	BIT 7,E	CBB0	RES 6,B
CB7C	BIT 7,H	CBB1	RES 6,C
CB7D	BIT 7,L	CBB2	RES 6,D
CB7E	BIT 7,(HL)	CBB3	RES 6,E
CBB4	RES 6,H	CBE9	SET 5,C
CBB5	RES 6,L	CBEA	SET 5,D
CBB6	RES 6,(HL)	CBEB	SET 5,E
CBB7	RES 6,A	CBEC	SET 5,H

MACHINE CODE	COMMAND	MACHINE CODE	COMMAND
CBB8	RES 7,B	CBED	SET 5,L
CBB9	RES 7,C	CBEE	SET 5,(HL)
CBBA	RES 7,D	CBEF	SET 5,A
CBBB	RES 7,E	CBF0	SET 6,B
CBBC	RES 7,H	CBF1	SET 6,C
CBBD	RES 7,L	CBF2	SET 6,D
CBBE	RES 7,(HL)	CBF3	SET 6,E
CBBF	RES 7,A	CBF4	SET 6,H
CBC0	SET 0,B	CBF5	SET 6,L
CBC1	SET 0,C	CBF6	SET 6,(HL)
CBC2	SET 0,D	CBF7	SET 6,A
CBC3	SET 0,E	CBF8	SET 7,B
CBC4	SET 0,H	CBF9	SET 7,C
CBC5	SET 0,L	CBFA	SET 7,D
CBC6	SET 0,(HL)	CBFB	SET 7,E
CBC7	SET 0,A	CBFC	SET 7,H
CBC8	SET 1,B	CBFD	SET 7,L
CBC9	SET 1,C	CBFE	SET 7,(HL)
CBCA	SET 1,D	CBFF	SET 7,A
CBCB	SET 1,E	DD09	ADD IX,BC
CBCC	SET 1,H	DD19	ADD IX+DE
CBCD	SET 1,L	DD218405	LD IX,NN
CBCE	SET 1,(HL)	DD228405	LD (NN),IX
CBCF	SET 1,A	DD23	INC IX
CBD0	SET 2,B	DD29	ADD IX,IX
CBD1	SET 2,C	DD2A8405	LD IX,(NN)
CBD2	SET 2,D	DD2B	DEC IX
CBD3	SET 2,E	DD3405	INC (IX+IND)
CBD4	SET 2,H	DD3505	DEC (IX+IND)
CBD5	SET 2,L	DD360520	LD (IX+IND),NN
CBD6	SET 2,(HL)	DD39	ADD IX,SP
CBD7	SET 2,A	DD4605	LD B,(IX+IND)
CBD8	SET 3,B	DD4E05	LD C,(IX+IND)
CBD9	SET 3,C	DD5605	LD D,(IX+IND)
CBDA	SET 3,D	DD5E05	LD E,(IX+IND)
CBDB	SET 3,E	DD6605	LD H,(IX+IND)
CBDC	SET 3,H	DD6E05	LD L,(IX+IND)
CBDD	SET 3,L	DD7005	LD (IX+IND),B
CBDE	SET 3,(HL)	DD7105	LD (IX+IND),C
CBDF	SET 3,A	DD7205	LD (IX+IND),D
CBE0	SET 4,B	DD7305	LD (IX+IND),E
CBE1	SET 4,C	DD7405	LD (IX+IND),H
CBE2	SET 4,D	DD7505	LD (IX+IND),L
CBE3	SET 4,E	DD7705	LD (IX+IND),A
CBE4	SET 4,H	DD7E05	LD A,(IX+IND)
CBE5	SET 4,L	DD8605	ADD A,(IX+IND)
CBE6	SET 4,(HL)	DD8E05	ADC A,(IX+IND)
CBE7	SET 4,A	DD9605	SUB (IX+IND)
CBE8	SET 5,B	DD9E05	SBC A,(IX+IND)
DDA605	AND (IX+IND)	ED50	IN D,(C)
DDAE05	XOR (IX+IND)	ED51	OUT (C),D
DDB605	XOR (IX+IND)	ED52	SBC HL,DE
DDBE05	CP (IX+IND)	ED538405	LD (NN),DE
DDE1	POP IX	ED56	IM 1
DDE3	EX (SP),IX	ED57	LD A,I
DDE5	PUSH IX	ED58	IN E,(C)
DDE9	JP (IX)	ED59	OUT (C),E

MACHINE CODE	COMMAND	MACHINE CODE	COMMAND
DDF9	LD SP,IX	ED5A	ADC HL,DE
DDCB0506	RLC (IX+IND)	ED5B8405	LD DE,(NN)
DDCB050E	RRC (IX+IND)	ED5E	IM 2
DDCB0516	RL (IX+IND)	ED60	IN H,(C)
DDCB051E	RR (IX+IND)	ED61	OUT (C),H
DDCB0526	SLA (IX+IND	ED62	SBC HL,HL
DDCB052E	SRA (IX+IND)	ED67	RRD
DDCB053E	SRL (IX+IND)	ED68	IN L,(C)
DDCB0546	BIT 0,(IX+IND)	ED69	OUT (C),L
DDCB054E	BIT 1,(IX+IND)	ED6A	ADC HL,HL
DDCB0556	BIT 2,(IX+IND)	ED6F	RLD
DDCB055E	BIT 3,(IX+IND)	ED72	SBC HL,SP
DDCB0566	BIT 4,(IX+IND)	ED738405	LD (NN),SP
DDCB056E	BIT 5,(IX+IND)	ED78	IN A,(C)
DDCB0576	BIT 6,(IX+IND)	ED79	OUT (C),A
DDCB057E	BIT 7,(IX+IND)	ED7A	ADC HL,SP
DDCB0586	RES 0,(IX+IND)	ED7B8405	LD SP,(NN)
DDCB058E	RES 1,(IX+IND)	EDA0	LDI
DDCB0596	RES 2,(IX+IND)	EDA1	CPI
DDCB059F	RES 3,(IX+IND)	EDA2	INI
DDCB05A6	RES 4,(IX+IND)	EDA3	OUTI
DDCB05AE	RES 5,(IX+IND)	EDA8	LDD
DDCB05B6	RES 6,(IX+IND)	EDA9	CPD
DDCB05BE	RES 7,(IX+IND)	EDAA	IND
DDCB05C6	SET 0,(IX+IND)	EDAB	OUTD
DDCB05CE	SET 1,(IX+IND)	EDB0	LDIR
DDCB05D6	SET 2,(IX+IND)	EDB1	CPIR
DDCB05DE	SET 3,(IX+IND)	EDB2	INIR
DDCB05E6	SET 4,(IX+IND)	EDB3	OTIR
DDCB05EE	SET 5,(IX+IND)	EDB8	LDDR
DDCB05F6	SET 6,(IX+IND)	EDB9	CPDR
DDCB05FE	SET 7,(IX+IND)	EDBA	INDR
ED40	IN B,(C)	EDBB	OTDR
ED41	OUT (C),B	FD09	ADD IY,BC
ED42	SBC HL,BC	FD19	ADD IY,DE
ED438405	LD (NN),BC	FD218405	LD IY,NN
ED44	NEG	FD228405	LD (NN),IY
ED45	RETN	FD23	INC IY
ED46	IM 0	FD29	ADD IY,IY
ED47	LD I,A	FD2A8405	LD IY,(NN)
ED48	IN C,(C)	FD2B	DEC IY
ED49	OUT (C),C	FD3405	INC (IY+IND)
ED4A	ADC HL,BC	FD3505	DEC (IY+IND)
ED4B8405	LD BC,(NN)	FD360520	LD (IY+IND),N
ED4D	RETI	FD39	ADD IY+SP
FD4605	LD B,(IY+IND)	FDCB05DE	SET 3,(IY+IND)
FD4E05	LD C,(IY+IND)	FDCB05E6	SET 4,(IY+IND)
FD5605	LD D,(IY+IND)	FDCB05EE	SET 5,(IY+IND)
FD5E05	LD E,(IY+IND)	FDCB05F6	SET 6,(IY+IND)
FD6605	LD H,(IY+IND)	FDCB05FE	SET 7,(IY+IND)
FD6E05	LD L,(IY+IND)		
FD7005	LD (IY+IND),B		
FD7105	LD (IY+IND),C		
FD7205	LD (IY+IND),D		
FD7305	LD (IY+IND),E		
FD7405	LD (IY+IND),H		
FD7505	LD (IY+IND),L		
FD7705	LD (IY+IND),A		

MACHINE CODE	COMMAND
FD7E05	LD A,(IY+IND)
FD8605	ADD A,(IY+IND)
FD8E05	ADC A,(IY+IND)
FD9605	SUB (IY+IND)
FD9E05	SBC A,(IY+IND)
FDA605	AND (IY+IND)
FDAE05	XOR (IY+IND)
FDB605	OR (IY+IND)
FDBE05	CP (IY+IND)
FDE1	POP IY
FDE3	EX (SP),IY
FDE5	PUSH IY
FDE9	JP (IY)
FDF9	LD SP,IY
FDCB0506	RLC (IY+IND)
FDCB050E	RRC (IY+IND)
FDCB0516	RL (IY+IND)
FDCB051E	RR (IY+IND)
FDCB0526	SLA (IY+IND)
FDCB052E	SRA (IY+IND)
FDCB053E	SRL (IY+IND)
FDCB0546	BIT 0,(IY+IND)
FDCB054E	BIT 1,(IY+IND)
FDCB0556	BIT 2,(IY+IND)
FDCB055E	BIT 3,(IY+IND)
FDCB0566	BIT 4,(IY+IND)
FDCB056E	BIT 5,(IY+IND)
FDCB0576	BIT 6,(IY+IND)
FDCB057E	BIT 7,(IY+IND)
FDCB0586	RES 0,(IY+IND)
FDCB058E	RES 1,(IY+IND)
FDCB0596	RES 2,(IY+IND)
FDCB059E	RES 3,(IY+IND)
FDCB05A6	RES 4,(IY+IND)
FDCB05AE	RES 5,(IY+IND)
FDCB05B6	RES 6,(IY+IND)
FDCB05BE	RES 7,(IY+IND)
FDCB05C6	SET 0,(IY+IND)
FDCB05CE	SET 1,(IY+IND)
FDCB05D6	SET 2,(IY+IND)

Appendix D
Alphabetic List of Machine Codes

COMMAND	CODE	COMMAND	CODE
ADC A,(HL)	8E	BIT 0,B	CB40
ADC A,(IX+IND)	DD8E05	BIT 0,C	CB41
ADC A,(IY+IND)	FD8E05	BIT 0,D	CB42
ADC A,A	8F	BIT 0,E	CB43
ADC A,B	88	BIT 0,H	CB44
ADC A,C	89	BIT 0,L	CB45
ADC A,D	8A	BIT 1,(HL)	CB4E
ADC A,E	8B	BIT 1,(IX+IND)	DDCB054E
ADC A,H	8C	BIT 1,(IY+IND)	FDCB054E
ADC A,L	8D	BIT 1,A	CB4F
ADC A,N	CE20	BIT 1,B	CB48
ADC HL,BC	ED4A	BIT 1,C	CB49
ADC HL,DE	ED5A	BIT 1,D	CB4A
ADC HL,HL	ED6A	BIT 1,E	CB4B
ADC HL,SP	ED7A	BIT 1,H	CB4C
ADD A,(HL)	86	BIT 1,L	CB4D
ADD A,(IX+IND)	DD8605	BIT 2,(HL)	CB56
ADD A,(IY+IND)	FD8605	BIT 2,(IX+IND)	DDCB0556
ADD A,A	87	BIT 2,(IY+IND)	FDCB0556
ADD A,B	80	BIT 2,A	CB57
ADD A,C	81	BIT 2,B	CB50
ADD A,D	82	BIT 2,C	CB51
ADD A,E	83	BIT 2,D	CB52
ADD A,H	84	BIT 2,E	CB53
ADD A,L	85	BIT 2,H	CB54
ADD A,N	C620	BIT 2,L	CB55
ADD HL,BC	09	BIT 3,(HL)	CB5E
ADD HL,DE	19	BIT 3,(IX+IND)	DDCB055E
ADD HL,HL	29	BIT 3,(IY+IND)	FDCB055E
ADD HL,SP	39	BIT 3,A	CB5F
ADD IX,BC	DD09	BIT 3,B	CB58
ADD IX,DE	DD19	BIT 3,C	CB59
ADD IX,IX	DD29	BIT 3,D	CB5A
ADD IX,SP	DD39	BIT 3,E	CB5B
ADD IY,BC	FD09	BIT 3,H	CB5C
ADD IY,DE	FD19	BIT 3,L	CB5D
ADD IY,IY	FD29	BIT 4,(HL)	CB66
ADD IY,SP	FD39	BIT 4,(IX+IND)	DDCB0566
AND (HL)	A6	BIT 4,(IY+IND)	FDCB0566
AND (IX+IND)	DDA605	BIT 4,A	CB67
AND (IY+IND)	FDA605	BIT 4,B	CB60
AND A	A7	BIT 4,C	CB61
AND B	A0	BIT 4,D	CB62
AND C	A1	BIT 4,E	CB63
AND D	A2	BIT 4,H	CB64
AND E	A3	BIT 4,L	CB65
AND H	A4	BIT 5,(HL)	CB6E
AND L	A5	BIT 5,(IX+IND)	DDCB056E
AND N	E620	BIT 5,(IY+IND)	FDCB056E
BIT 0,(HL)	CB46	BIT 5,A	CB6F
BIT 0,(IX+IND)	DDCB0546	BIT 5,B	CB68
BIT 0,(IY+IND)	FDCB0546	BIT 5,C	CB69
BIT 0,A	CB47	BIT 5,D	CB6A

COMMAND	CODE	COMMAND	CODE
-------	----	-------	----
BIT 5.E	CB6B	DEC IY	FD2B
BIT 5.H	CB6C	DEC L	2D
BIT 5.L	CB6D	DEC SP	3B
BIT 6,(HL)	CB76	DI	F3
BIT 6,(IX+IND)	DDCB0576	DJNZ DIS	102E
BIT 6,(IY+IND)	FDCB0576	EI	FB
BIT 6.A	CB77	EX (SP).HL	E3
BIT 6.B	CB70	EX (SP).IX	DDE3
BIT 6.C	CB71	EX (SP).IY	FDE3
BIT 6.D	CB72	EX AF.AF'	08
BIT 6.E	CB73	EX DE,HL	EB
BIT 6.H	CB74	EXX	D9
BIT 6.L	CB75	HALT	76
BIT 7,(HL)	CB7E	IM 0	ED46
BIT 7,(IX+IND)	DDCB057E	IM 1	ED56
BIT 7,(IY+IND)	FDCB057E	IM 2	ED5E
BIT 7.A	CB7F	IN A,(C)	ED78
BIT 7.B	CB78	IN A.N	DB20
BIT 7.C	CB79	IN B,(C)	ED40
BIT 7.D	CB7A	IN C,(C)	ED48
BIT 7.E	CB7B	IN D,(C)	ED50
BIT 7.H	CB7C	IN E,(C)	ED58
BIT 7.L	CB7D	IN H,(C)	ED60
CALL C.NN	DC8405	IN L,(C)	ED68
CALL M,NN	FC8405	INC (HL)	34
CALL NC,NN	D48405	INC (IX+IND)	DD3405
CALL NN	CD8405	INC (IY+IND)	FD3405
CALL NZ.NN	C48405	INC A	3C
CALL P,NN	F48405	INC B	04
CALL PE.NN	EC8405	INC BC	03
CALL PO.NN	E48405	INC C	0C
CALL Z,NN	CC8405	INC D	14
CCF	3F	INC DE	13
CP (HL)	BE	INC E	1C
CP (IX+IND)	DDBE05	INC H	24
CP (IY+IND)	FDBE05	INC HL	23
CP A	BF	INC IX	DD23
CP B	B8	INC IY	FD23
CP C	B9	INC L	2C
CP D	BA	INC SP	33
CP E	BB	IND	EDAA
CP H	BC	INDR	EDBA
CP L	BD	INI	EDA2
CP N	FE20	INIR	EDB2
CPD	EDA9	JP (HL)	E9
CPDR	EDB9	JP (IX)	DDE9
CPI	EDA1	JP (IY)	FDE9
CPIR	EDB1	JP C,NN	DA8405
CPL	2F	JP M,NN	FA8405
DAA	27	JP NC,NN	D28405
DEC (HL)	35	JP NN	C38405
DEC (IX+IND)	DD3505	JP NZ.NN	C28405
DEC A	3D	JP P,NN	F28405
DEC B	05	JP PE,NN	EA8405
DEC BC	0B	JP PO,NN	E28405
DEC C	0D	JP Z,NN	CA8405
DEC D	15	JR C,DIS	382E
DEC DE	1B	JR DIS	182E
DEC E	1D	JR NC,DIS	302E
DEC H	25	JR NZ,DIS	202E
DEC HL	2B	JR Z,DIS	282E
DEC IX	DD2B	LD (BC),A	02

COMMAND	CODE	COMMAND	CODE
LD (DE),A	12	LD C,A	4F
LD (HL),A	77	LD C,B	48
LD (HL),B	70	LD C,C	49
LD (HL),C	71	LD C,D	4A
LD (HL),D	72	LD C,E	4B
LD (HL),E	73	LD C,H	4C
LD (HL),H	74	LD C,L	4D
LD (HL),N	3620	LD C,N	0E20
LD (IX+IND),A	DD7705	LD D,(HL)	56
LD (IX+IND),B	DD7005	LD D,(IX+IND)	DD5605
LD (IX+IND),C	DD7105	LD D,(IY+IND)	FD5605
LD (IX+IND),D	DD7205	LD D,A	57
LD (IX+IND),E	DD7305	LD D,B	50
LD (IX+IND),H	DD7405	LD D.C	51
LD (IX+IND),L	DD7505	LD D,D	52
LD (IX+IND),N	DD360520	LD D,E	53
LD (IY+IND),A	FD7705	LD D,H	54
LD (IY+IND),B	FD7005	LD D,L	55
LD (IY+IND),C	FD7105	LD D,N	1620
LD (IY+IND),D	FD7205	LD DE,(NN)	ED5B8405
LD (IY+IND),E	FD7305	LD DE,NN	118405
LD (IY+IND),H	FD7405	LD D,(HL)	5E
LD (IY+IND),L	FD7505	LD E,(IX+IND)	DDE505
LD (IY+IND),N	FD360520	LD E,(IY+IND)	FDE505
LD (NN),A	328405	LD E,A	5F
LD (NN),BC	ED438405	LD E,B	58
LD (NN),DE	ED538405	LD E,C	59
LD (NN),HL	228405	LD E,D	5A
LD (NN),IX	DD228405	LD E,E	5B
LD (NN),IY	FD228405	LD E,H	5C
LD (NN),SP	ED738405	LD E,L	5D
LD A,(BC)	0A	LD E,N	1E20
LD A,(DE)	1A	LD H,(HL)	66
LD A,(HL)	7E	LD H,(IX+IND)	DD6605
LD A,(IX+IND)	DD7E05	LD H,(IY+IND)	FD6605
LD A,(IY+IND)	FD7E05	LD H,A	67
LD A,(NN)	3A8405	LD H,B	60
LD A,A	7F	LD H,C	61
LD A,B	78	LD H,D	62
LD A,C	79	LD H,E	63
LD A,D	7A	LD H,H	64
LD A,E	7B	LD H,L	65
LD A,H	7C	LD H,N	2620
LD A,I	ED57	LD HL,(NN)	2A8405
LD A,L	7D	LD HL,NN	218405
LD A,N	3E20	LD I,A	ED47
LD B,(HL)	46	LD IX,(NN)	DD2A8405
LD B,(IX+IND)	DD4605	LD IX,NN	DD218405
LD B,(IY+IND)	FD4605	LD IY,(NN)	FD2A8405
LD B,A	47	LD IY,NN	FD218405
LD B,B	40	LD L,(HL)	6E
LD B,C	41	LD L,(IX+IND)	DD6E05
LD B,D	42	LD L,(IY+IND)	FD6E05
LD B,E	43	LD L,A	6F
LD B,H,NN	44	LD L,B	68
LD B,L	45	LD L,C	69
LD B,N	0620	LD L,D	6A
LD BC,(NN)	ED4B8405	LD L,E	6B
LD BC,NN	018405	LD L,H	6C
LD C,(HL)	4E	LD L,L	6D
LD C,(IX+IND)	DD4E05	LD L,N	2E20
LD C,(IY+IND)	FD4E05	LD SP,(NN)	ED7B8405

COMMAND	CODE	COMMAND	CODE
LD SP,HL	F9	RES 1,E	CB8B
LD SP,IX	DDF9	RES 1,H	CB8C
LD SP,IY	FDF9	RES 1,L	CB8D
LD SP,NN	318405	RES 2,(HL)	CB96
LDD	EDA8	RES 2,(IX+IND)	DDCB0596
LDDR	EDB8	RES 2,(IY+IND)	FDCB0596
LDI	EDA0	RES 2,A	CB97
LDIR	EDB0	RES 2,B	CB90
NEG	ED44	RES 2,C	CB91
NOP	00	RES 2,D	CB92
OR (HL)	B6	RES 2,E	CB93
OR (IX+IND)	DDB605	RES 2,H	CB94
OR (IY+IND)	FDB605	RES 2,L	CB95
OR A	B7	RES 3,(HL)	CB9E
OR B	B0	RES 3,(IX+IND)	DDCB059E
OR C	B1	RES 3,(IY+IND)	FDCB059E
OR D	B2	RES 3,A	CB9F
OR E	B3	RES 3,B	CB98
OR H	B4	RES 3,C	CB99
OR L	B5	RES 3,D	CB9A
OR N	F620	RES 3,E	CB9B
OTDR	EDBB	RES 3,H	CB9C
OTIR	EDB3	RES 3,L	CB9D
OUT (C),A	ED79	RES 4,(HL)	CBA6
OUT (C),B	ED41	RES 4,(IX+IND)	DDCB05A6
OUT (C),C	ED49	RES 4,A	CBA7
OUT (C),D	ED51	RES 4,B	CBA0
OUT (C),E	ED59	RES 4,C	CBA1
OUT (C),H	ED61	RES 4,D	CBA2
OUT (C),L	ED69	RES 4,E	CBA3
OUT N,A	DE20	RES 4,H	CBA4
OUTD	EDA8	RES 4,L	CBA5
OUTI	EDA3	RES 5,(HL)	CBAE
POP AF	F1	RES 5,(IX+IND)	DDCB05AE
POP BC	C1	RES 5,(IY+IND)	FDCB05AE
POP DE	D1	RES 5,A	CBAF
POP HL	E1	RES 5.B	CBA8
POP IX	DDE1	RES 5,C	CBA9
FOP IY	FDE1	RES 5,D	CBAA
PUSF AF	F5	RES 5,E	CBAB
PUSH BC	C5	RES 5,H	CBAC
PUSH DE	D5	RES 5,L	CBAD
PUSH HL	E5	RES 6,(HL)	CBB6
PUSH IX	DDE5	RES 6,(IX+IND)	DDCB05B6
PUSH IY	FDE5	RES 6,(IY+IND)	FDCB05B6
RES 0,(HL)	CB86	RES 6,A	CBB7
RES 0,(IX+IND)	DDCB0586	RES 6,B	CBB0
RES 0,(IY+IND)	FDCB0586	RES 6,C	CBB1
RES 0,A	CB87	RES 6,D	CBB2
RES 0,B	CB80	RES 6,E	CBB3
RES 0,C	CB81	RES 6,H	CBB4
RES 0,D	CB82	RES 6,L	CBB5
RES 0,E	CB83	RES 7,(HL)	CBBE
RES 0,H	CB84	RES 7,(IX+IND)	DDCB05BE
RES 0,L	CB85	RES 7,(IY+IND)	FDCB05BE
RES 1,(HL)	CB8E	RES 7,A	CBBF
RES 1,(IX+IND)	DDCB058E	RES 7,B	CBB8
RES 1,(IY+IND)	FDCB058E	RES 7,C	CBB9
RES 1,A	CB8F	RES 7,D	CBBA
RES 1,B	CB88	RES 7,E	CBBB
RES 1,C	CB89	RES 7,H	CBBC
RES 1,D	CB8A	RES 7,L	CBBD

COMMAND	CODE	COMMAND	CODE
RET	C9	RST 30H	F7
RET C	D8	RST 38H	FF
RET M	F8	RST 8	CF
RET NC	D0	SBC A,(HL)	9E
RET NZ	C0	SBC A,(IX+IND)	DD9E05
RET P	F0	SBC A,(IY+IND)	FD9E05
RET PE	E8	SBC A,A	9F
RET PO	E0	SBC A,B	98
RET Z	C8	SBC A,C	99
RETI	ED4D	SBC A,D	9A
RETN	ED45	SBC A,E	9B
RL (HL)	CB16	SBC A,H	9C
RL (IX+IND)	DDCB0516	SBC A,L	9D
RL (IY+IND)	FDCB0516	SBC A,N	DE20
RL A	CB17	SBC HL,BC	ED42
RL B	CB10	SBC HL,DE	ED52
RL C	CB11	SBC HL,HL	ED62
RL D	CB12	SBC HL,SP	ED72
RL E	CB13	SCF	37
RL H	CB14	SET 0,(HL)	CBC6
RL L	CB15	SET 0,(IX+IND)	DDCB05C6
RLA	17	SET 0,(IY+IND)	FDCB05C6
RLC (HL)	CB06	SET 0,A	CBC7
RLC (IX+IND)	DDCB0506	SET 0,B	CBC0
RLC (IY+IND)	FDCB0506	SET 0,C	CBC1
RLC A	CB07	SET 0,D	CBC2
RLC B	CB00	SET 0,E	CBC3
RLC C	CB01	SET 0,H	CBC4
RLC D	CB02	SET 0,L	CBC5
RLC E	CB03	SET 1,(HL)	CBCE
RLC H	CB04	SET 1,(IX+IND)	DDCB05CE
RLC L	CB05	SET 1,(IY+IND)	FDCB05CE
RLCA	07	SET 1,A	CBCF
RLD	ED6F	SET 1,B	CBC8
RR (HL)	CB1E	SET 1,C	CBC9
RR (IX+IND)	DDCB051E	SET 1,D	CBCA
RR (IY+IND)	FDCB051E	SET 1,E	CBCB
RR A	CB1F	SET 1,H	CBCC
RR B	CB18	SET 1,L	CBCD
RR C	CB19	SET 2,(HL)	CBD6
RR D	CB1A	SET 2,(IX+IND)	DDCB05D6
RR E	CB1B	SET 2,(IY+IND)	FDCB05D6
RR H	CB1C	SET 2,A	CBD7
RR L	CB1D	SET 2,B	CBD0
RRA	1F	SET 2,C	CBD1
RRC (HL)	CB0E	SET 2,D	CBD2
RRC (IX+IND)	DDCB050E	SET 2,E	CBD3
RRC (IY+IND)	FDCB050E	SET 2,H	CBD4
RRC A	CB0F	SET 2,L	CBD5
RRC B	CB08	SET 3,B	CBD8
RRC C	CB09	SET 3,(HL)	CBDE
RRC D	CB0A	SET 3,(IX+IND)	DDCB05DE
RRC E	CB0B	SET 3,(IY+IND)	FDCB05DE
RRC H	CB0C	SET 3,A	CBDF
RRC L	CB0D	SET 3,C	CBD9
RRCA	0F	SET 3,D	CBDA
RRD	ED67	SET 3,E	CBDB
RST 0	C7	SET 3,H	CBDC
RST 10H	D7	SET 3,L	CBDD
RST 18H	DF	SET 4,(HL)	CBE6
RST 20H	E7	SET 4,(IX+IND)	DDCB05E6
RST 28H	EF	SET 4,(IY+IND)	FDCB05E6

COMMAND	CODE
SET 4,A	CBE7
SET 4,B	CBE0
SET 4,C	CBE1
SET 4,D	CBE2
SET 4,E	CBE3
SET 4,H	CBE4
SET 4,L	CBE5
SET 5,(HL)	CBEE
SET 5,(IX+IND)	DDCB05EE
SET 5,(IY+IND)	FDCB05EE
SET 5,A	CBEF
SET 5,B	CBE8
SET 5,C	CBE9
SET 5,D	CBEA
SET 5,E	CBEB
SET 5,H	CBEC
SET 5,L	CBED
SET 6,(HL)	CBF6
SET 6,(IX+IND)	DDCB05F6
SET 6,(IY+IND)	FDCB05F6
SET 6,A	CBF5
SET 6,B	CBF0
SET 6,C	CBF1
SET 6,D	CBF2
SET 6,E	CBF3
SET 6,H	CBF4
SET 6,L	CBF5
SET 7,(HL)	CBFE
SET 7,(IX+IND)	DDCB05FE
SET 7,(IY+IND)	FDCB05FE
SET 7,A	CBFF
SET 7,B	CBF8
SET 7,C	CBF9
SET 7,D	CBFA
SET 7,E	CBFB
SET 7,H	CBFC
SET 7,L	CBFD
SLA (HL)	CB26
SLA (IX+IND)	DDCB0526
SLA (IY+IND)	FDCB0526
SLA A	CB27
SLA B	CB20
SLA C	CB21
SLA D	CB22
SLA E	CB23

COMMAND	CODE
SLA H	CB24
SLA L	CB25
SRA (HL)	CB2E
SRA (IX+IND)	DDCB052E
SRA (IY+IND)	FDCB052E
SRA A	CB2F
SRA B	CB28
SRA C	CB29
SRA D	CB2A
SRA E	CB2B
SRA H	CB2C
SRA L	CB2D
SRL (HL)	CB3E
SRL (IX+IND)	DDCB053E
SRL (IY+IND)	FDCB053E
SRL A	CB3F
SRL B	CB38
SRL C	CB39
SRL D	CB3A
SRL E	CB3B
SRL H	CB3C
SRL L	CB3D
SUB (HL)	96
SUB (IX+IND)	DD9605
SUB (IY+IND)	FD9605
SUB A	97
SUB B	90
SUB C	91
SUB D	92
SUB E	93
SUB H	94
SUB L	95
SUB N	D620
XOR (HL)	AE
XOR (IX+IND)	DDAE05
XOR (IY+IND)	FDAE05
XOR A	AF
XOR B	A8
XOR C	A9
XOR D	AA
XOR E	AB
XOR H	AC
XOR L	AD
XOR N	EE20

Appendix E Reserved Words

The following is a list of reserved words that are used for op-codes, and CANNOT BE USED FOR LABELS.

LD	AND	RLA	DJNZ
PUSH	OR	RRCA	CALL
POP	XOR	RRA	RET
EX	CP	RLC	RETI
EXX	INC	RL	RETN
LDI	DEC	RRC	RST
LDIR	DAA	RR	IN
LDD	CPL	SLA	INI
LDDR	NEG	SRA	INIR
CPI	CCF	SRL	IND
CPIR	SCF	RLD	INDR
CPD	NOP	RRD	OUT
CPDR	HALT	BIT	OUTI
ADD	DI	SET	OTIR
ADC	EI	RES	OUTD
SUB	IM	JP	OTDR
SBC	RLCA	JR	

Glossary

Glossary

address—A memory location that holds a value and instruction.
alphanumerics—A combination of letters and numbers.
analogous—Performed by using definite values.
assembly—A type of computer language that takes a written instruction and converts it to the proper machine code.
BASIC—A computer language. This is the language that the TRS-80 comes programmed in. It must be converted to machine language before execution.
binary—A numbering system that uses powers of 2 and contains only 2 digits.
bit—The smallest unit in a memory location.
block—A group of bytes or memory locations.
bomb—Fail or return to power up condition.
buffer—A special area set aside to store information in.
byte—A piece of information or the contents of a memory location. Also sometimes referred to as a memory location.
CALL—To branch to, or go to another part of a program and have a method of returning to the next instruction after the call.
character—Any of the letters or numbers on the keyboard. Equal to one byte.

compiler—A program or device used to translate information from one language to machine code.

decimal—Power of 10.

hexadecimal—Power of 16.

increment—To increase by one.

jump—To move from one routine to another while skipping over other instructions. This command does not include a return.

label—A group of alphanumerics that begin with a letter and provides a name for the routine.

load—To store a value somewhere or in something.

machine—A type of programming language.

one's complement—One at a time.

op-code—Operation code.

operand—The register, register pair, or location that the operation is being performed on.

parity—Quality of being equal.

POP—To retrieve from the stack.

powers—Numbers of times a number is to be multiplied.

pseudo-op—A special operational command.

PUSH—To save the contents of a register pair on the top of the stack.

RAM—Random access memory.

register—A container or carrier of information.

reset—To change the contents of a bit from 1 to 0.

shift—To move the contents of a register.

stack—The available memory above the last program instruction.

two's complement—Two at a time.

Index

Index

A

Abbreviations, 24
Accumulator, 31
ADC command, 68, 84
ADD, special, 68
ADD commands, 66, 83, 85
Addition, 65
Addresses, 13
Add /subtract flag, 58
ADD with CARRY command, 68, 84
AF register pair, 58
AND command, 69
A register, 58
Assembly language, ix, 11
Assembly language conversion to machine language, 17

B

BASIC, ix, 11, 17
BASIC conversion to machine language, 163
BCD, 77
Binary coded decimal, 77
Binary division, 5
Binary numbers, 1, 2
Binary-to-decimal conversion, 2, 4
Bit, 27
BIT command, 97
Block transfers, 54
Buffer, 24
Buffers, 118
Byte, 27

C

CALL command, 111
Carry flag, 58
CCF command, 79
Central processing unit, 11
C flag, 58
Character codes, 173
COBOL 9, ix
Comment, 19
COMPARE commands, 59, 72
Compilers, 17, 163
CONDITIONAL CALL, 112
CONDITIONAL RETURN, 112
Condition flag, 58
Copying of programs, 12
CPD command, 61
CPDR op-code, 61
CPI command, 59
CPIR op-code, 61
CPL command, 78
CPU, 11

D

Data retrieval, 47
Data transferal, 126, 130
DEC, 72, 85
Decimal numbers, 1
Decimal to hexadecimal conversion, 6
DECREMENT command, 72, 85
DEFB pseudo-op, 117
DEFINE LABEL pseudo-op, 117
DEFINE MESSAGE pseudo-op, 118
DEFINE SPACE pseudo-op, 118
DEFINE WORD pseudo-op, 117
DEFINITE BYTE pseudo-op, 117

DEFL pseudo-op, 117
DEFM pseudo-op, 118
DEFS pseudo-op, 118
DEFW pseudo-op,
Displacement back from end of command, 175
DISPLACEMENT jump on non zero, 106
Division, 65
DJNZ command, 106
Driver, 126

E

Editor /Assembler, 12, 17
English language, ix
EQUATE pseudo-op, 117
EQU pseudo-op, 117
EX, 51
EXCHANGE command, 51
EXCLUSIVE OR command, 71

F

Flag, condition, 37, 58
Flags, 58
FORTRAN, ix
F register, 37, 58, 79

H

Half carry flag, 58
Hard copy of memory location contents program, 139
Hard copy program,
Hex. *See* hexidecimal numbers,
Hexadecimal numbers, 1, 5
Hexadecimal to decimal conversion, 7
Hex control codes, 173
H flag, 58
HL register pair, 39

I

INC command, 72, 85
INCREMENT command, 72, 85
INE pseudo-op, 116
INPUT command group, 111
Interpreters, 17
Interrupts, 34, 61
Interrupt vector, 34
IX register pair, 14, 30
IY register pair, 14, 30

J

JR command, 105
JUMP command, 103
JUMP relevant command, 105

K

Key codes, 173

L

Labels, 19
Languages, computer, ix
LDD instruction, 56
LDI instruction, 54
LD op-code, 27
LIFO, 23
Line numbers, 18
Load, 27
LOAD commands, combinations of, 51
LOGICAL ADD operation, 71
LOGICAL AND operation, 69
Lowercase codes, 174

M

Machine code, 18
Machine language, ix, 11
Mailing list program, 132
Masking, 70
Mathematical functions, 65, 83
Memory, 23
Memory, read-only, 14
Memory locations, 13
Memory stack, 23
Multiplication, 65

N

N, 24
NEG command, 78
N flag, 58
no-op command, 79
NOP command, 79
Numbering systems, 1

O

Op-code, 19
Operand, 19
Operation code, 19
OR command, 70
ORG pseudo-op, 115
ORIGINATE pseudo-op, 115
OUTPUT command group, 111

P

Parity /overflow flag, 58
PC command, 61
PL /I, ix
POP command, 45
Powers of 10 table, 2
Program counter, 61
Programming, ix
Program time, 11
Pseudo-op, 19, 115
PUSH command, 44
P/V flag, 58

Q

Quick Printer II, 126

R

R, 24
R′, 24
Refresh memory, 34
Register pair, 14
Register pairs, special, 14
Registers, 13
Register types, 14
RETURN commands, 112
RLA instruction, 89
RLCA instruction, 89
RL instruction, 9
ROM, 14
ROTATE, 89
Rotate left arithmetic, 90
Rotate left instruction, 91
Rotate left with carry arithmetic, 89
Rotate right arithmetic, 91
Rotate right instruction, 93
Rotate right with carry arithmetic, 90
Rotate right with carry instruction, 92
RR, 24
RR′, 24
RRA, 91
RRCA instruction, 90
RRC instruction, 91
RR instruction, 93

S

SBC command, 69, 84
SCF command, 79
Screen, clearing the, 123, 125
Screen, filling with one character, 128
Searches, 57
Searching by comparison, 9, 58
SET instruction, 98
S flag, 59
SHIFT instructions, 93
Shift left arithmetic instruction, 93
Shift right arithmetic instruction, 93
Sign flag, 59
SLA instruction, 93
SP register pair, 37
SRA instruction, 93
Stack, internal, 24
Stack, memory, 23
Stack pointer, 14, 43
Stack pointer register pair, 37
SUB command, 68
Subroutines, 12
Subtraction, 65
Subtraction commands, 68
SUBTRACT with CARRY 9, 69, 84
System tape, program for copying, 150

T

T-BUG program, 12, 18

U

UNCONDITIONAL CALL, 111
UNCONDITIONAL RETURN, 112

X

XOR command, 71

Z

Zero flag, 59
Z flag, 59